THE COMPLETE GUIDE TO THE GREAT DANE

Mal Lee

LP Media Inc. Publishing

Text copyright © 2020 by LP Media Inc.

www.lpmedia.org

Publication Data

Mal Lee

The Complete Guide to the Great Dane ---- First edition.

Summary: "Successfully raising a Great Dane Dog from puppy to old age" --- Provided by publisher.

ISBN: 978-1-952069-03-1

[1.Great Dane Dogs --- Non-Fiction] I. Title.

Design by Sorin Rădulescu

First paperback edition, 2020

TABLE OF CONTENTS

INTRODUCTION
The Big Three

Jax as a Puppy

I remember the first time I ever came nose to nose with a Great Dane. My wife and I were newly married and in the process of buying a car.

We found what we were looking for in the classifieds (no eBay in the early '80s!) and went to the seller's house.

Knocking on the front door, we were met with an extremely deep bark. The door swung open, and there stood a handsome, albeit huge Great Dane.

Blue, named after his coat color, was the most impressive dog we had ever seen. He was gentle, obedient, and the perfect representation of this giant breed.

Both dog lovers, we vowed that one day when we were financially able to, we would make a Great Dane a member of our family.

Five years later, with our own PR business (which meant we could take a puppy to work with us!), we moved into a house that included its own orchard. Its huge outside space was ideal, and so we decided to adopt a rescue Great Dane to join our two mixed-breed dogs, Boo (Chihuahua cross breed) and Huggy Bear (Sheepdog cross breed).

Our vet put us in touch with a Great Dane rescue center in Wales. But before we could apply to be adopters, we had to pass the Great Dane test!

This trial by Danes meant standing in a field surrounded by 15-20 huge stampeding dogs.

The center manager told us that this "test" eliminates more than half of the prospective applicants! And it was agreed that as we weren't put off by the sheer size of these colossal canines, we could move on to the next step—the home visit.

Passing the home visit, we went on to adopt Arnold.

At around six years of age, Arnold, a senior dog, had not had a great life and wasn't with us for nearly long enough. I will talk more about Arnold and our other Great Danes throughout this book. Suffice to say, Arnold is responsible for my family's ongoing love of this breed.

When a Great Dane passes, it leaves a massive hole in your heart and your home. So it wasn't long before we adopted the energetic, six-month-old adolescent dog, Billy Ray. This canine addition to our family was followed by the birth of our daughter, Mikki, some 18 months later.

The years passed as Billy and Mikki became inseparable. He grew from adolescent to senior, as she grew from baby to toddler.

When Billy Ray passed due to kidney failure, at a little over six years of age, we moved closer to the city and decided to take a break from Great Dane ownership.

Jax Age 8

Just over a decade later, Jax Teller, a ten-week-old Great Dane, joined our family.

This time we decided to bite the bullet and choose a puppy rather than senior or adolescent dog.

At 17, Mikki volunteered to be in charge of training and socializing Jax. So, in the summer of 2012, Jax joined our family and became a companion to our ten-year-old Field Spaniel, Cocoa Pop.

Cocoa passed in 2014, and when we decided to move to Greece a year later, there was no question that Jax would come with us.

At over seven years of age, Jax is beginning to wind down. He may now have a graying muzzle

Mikki and Billy Ray 1997

and be a little stiff, but he remains Alpha of his pack. His little gang consists of Gumbo, our adopted Pit Bull cross breed, and Beanie, a small rescue Greek hunting dog. Both rescue center dogs we gave a forever home to since our move to Greece.

Jax now spends most days lying in the sun and playing nursemaid to the many pups and abandoned dogs that my family fosters while they wait to travel to their forever homes.

My experiences with the Big Three—Arnold, Billy Ray, and Jax Teller—are the inspiration behind this book.

CHAPTER 1
An Introduction to Great Danes

Great Dane History

"I believe the Great Dane is the closest breed to human in terms of personality and heart. My dogs are expressive, loving, and living with them is truly more humorous at times than one can imagine."

Nathan Bolby
Grand Mimeux

Photo Courtesy of
Sam and Danny Dowsett

Whether you're planning on adopting a Corgi or a Cane Corso, a Dachshund or a Dane, it's a good idea to do your homework.

As the old saying goes, A dog is for life, not just for Christmas.

Remember, this new addition is likely to be with you for a long time. The relationship could last for six years—as it did with my first Great Dane, Arnold, or 20, like Gem the Chihuahua, my first childhood pet. Consider this: the longest living dog in the world, Australian Cattle Dog Bluey, lived to the ripe old age of 29!

HELPFUL TIP
A Great Match?

The Great Dane is a mild-mannered, easygoing dog that needs only a moderate amount of exercise. With a very low, loud bark and a colorful, easily maintained coat, Great Danes are known as "gentle giants" by many of their owners. Although jumping is considered an adverse characteristic, potential Dane owners should be advised that this breed is also known for drooling, slobbering, and a short life span.

So before we go any further, let's take a look at the fascinating history of the mighty Great Dane.

There are a few different versions of the history of these magnificent dogs. Some say the evolution of the breed began several centuries ago in Britain, while others argue their origins lie firmly in Germany.

One thing is sure though, dogs resembling Danes feature in Egyptian carvings dating back to 3000 BC.

By the fifth century, the Alani, responsible for invading Europe, brought with them giant Mastiff dogs. Some also believe the Romans are to thank for bringing Mastiffs to Europe.

It was the Celts, however, who several hundred years later, cross-bred these giants with Irish Wolfhounds or Grey Hounds (sometimes even both) to create the English Dogge—a giant yet slimmer version of the pure Mastiff, whom many believe to be the modern-day Great Dane's ancestor.

Fast forward to the 16th century, when Germany imported a large number of English Dogges for cross breeding as they strove to create the perfect Boar Hunter. European wild boars were ferocious, and hunting them required a dog that was strong, fast, and aggressive.

The Great Danes of days gone by were huge, ferocious, capable of tracking, and explicitly bred to hunt, with cropped ears to prevent them from being torn by boar tusks.

The Germans soon realized that a dog of these proportions would also make an ideal guard dog. To fulfill this role though, it would need to be more tame and personable.

To this end, by the 18th and 19th centuries, dog breeders in Germany worked hard to evolve the Boar Hound into a breed with a good temperament. By 1880, German breeders and dog show judges agreed that this new breed was so different from the Mastiff that it was formally declared the Deutsche Doggen.

Eleven years later saw the forming of the Great Dane Club of Germany and the adoption of today's standard. By 1899, the Great Dane Club of America (GDCA) was formed in Chicago, and the Great Dane gained North American recognition.

So how does a dog with no historical ties to Denmark get the title Great Dane? We can thank 18th-century French naturalist and mathematician Comte de Buffon, who first came across these dogs during his travels through Denmark. Comte gave the breed the name "le Grande Denois," or Great Dane. For some strange reason, in English anyway, this name stuck, tying the dog to Denmark forevermore.

And the rest, as they say, is history!

Photo Courtesy of Brandi Bigelow

Great Dane Fun Facts

For some, the Great Dane conjures up an image of its lovable cartoon counterpart, Scooby-Doo, the endearing albeit clumsy canine who solved ghostly mysteries with his human gang. In fact, a Great Dane is full of spirit, and despite its huge size, should be neither clumsy nor fearful.

The Great Dane is a loyal companion and the perfect pet for anyone prepared to spend lots of quality time with their dog. They are powerful yet personable and well deserve their gentle giant reputation.

Here are some fun facts to help you learn a little bit more about this most amazing of K9 companions:

- During World War II, both the marines and the army attempted to train Great Danes for battle, but none of them passed the basic training!
- President Franklin D. Roosevelt always had several Great Danes close by.
- The famous Red Baron took his Dane, Moritz, along with him on a couple of flights.
- In the Middle Ages, it was thought that Great Danes could ward away evil spirits and so they roamed free on their owners' land.
- The famous cartoon "Scooby-Doo," featuring a reluctant ghost-hunting Dane, was originally entitled "Too Much."
- The Tallest Dog in the World Ever title goes to Great Dane Zeus, who stood 44 inches tall at his withers and 88 inches when standing on his hind legs. Zeus sadly passed away in 2014.
- Buffalo Bill Cody always had his black Great Dane, Turk, by his side.
- In August 2019, King Rama X of Thailand rescued 15 starving and skeletal Great Danes from an abandoned breeding farm. His Majesty pledged to cover all treatment, food, and care costs.
- The Great Dane Juliana holds not one but two Blue Cross medals. The first for her actions in 1941, when, awoken by a bomb falling on her home, she defused it by peeing on it! The second, three years later, for alerting the authorities to a fire in her owner's shoe shop.
- According to established dream interpreters, if you dream of a Great Dane then it's a reminder not to allow people to manipulate or take advantage of you.
- The Great Dane is Pennsylvania's Official State Dog.
- The average life span of a Great Dane is 6-8 years.
- Adam West, aka the first actor to play Batman, was the proud owner of a Great Dane named Batdog.

Photo Courtesy of Carmel Huppert

Physical Characteristics

"Their size is what grabs people's immediate attention. But when you get to know the breed their devotion to their owners is unlike any other breed. The love these dogs give to their people is even more impressive than their stature."

Brandy Massey
Massey Great Danes

The Great Dane's overall appearance is one of elegance and strength. Its smooth and well-formed muscular body characterizes this giant breed.

Danes are huge but not bulky. Their powerful gait has a long reach and is never clumsy.

A well-trained Dane will be friendly, loyal, dependable, and spirited. This dog is always imposing but never aggressive or nervous. It is this combination that gives the breed its gentle giant title.

Let's take a look at a Great Dane's overall appearance:

Head: Great Danes have huge heads that are long and rectangular. The line of the muzzle and the line of the top of the skull should be straight and almost parallel. Overall the head should give the dog an expressive, distinguished, and majestic appearance. A female Dane's head will be more delicate than that of the male.

Eyes: Most Danes have light or dark brown eyes except for Harlequins or Blues, who can have blue eyes. Eyes should be intelligent, of medium size, and deep-set. Eyelids should be relatively tight and almond shaped, and brows should be well developed.

Ears: Cropped ears should be proportionate to the size of the dog's head and uniformly erect. Non-cropped ears should be medium-sized, moderately thick, and high-set. They should be folded forward and close to the cheek.

Nose: The majority of adult Danes have a black nose, but this can differ depending on the dog's coat. For example, a Blue Dane very often has a dark blue-black nose, while a Harlequin's is spotted.

Body: The Dane's neck is ideally high-set, long, muscular, and arched. From the nape of the neck, it should gradually broaden and flow into the ridge between the shoulder blades (the withers). The chest should be deep, broad, and muscular, with the front part having a pronounced breastbone. You should be able to easily feel your dog's ribs, but they shouldn't protrude. The top line of the Dane's hindquarters should be broad and slightly sloping. While some Danes are stockier than others, overall, you are looking for the outline of your dog's body to resemble an hourglass shape.

Legs And Paws: A Dane should have long and straight front legs with broad and muscular hind legs. Danes have large paws. Their toes are well-arched and around the size of an average man's splayed hand. Nails should be strong, short, and dark.

Tail: The tail, if not docked, will be of moderate length (33"-36"long), thick and tapering toward its hind legs. It should be high set and level with the top line. We will explore the pros and cons of tail docking in a later chapter.

Now that we know what we are looking for regarding your Great Dane's body, let's move on to coat expectations.

Photo Courtesy of
Estelle Burton

Coat And Color Variations

"Great Danes come in all colors from harlequin (spotted), fawn, brindle, merle and many more. It is not often you find a breed that has so many color variations."

Shawna Howard
Cottonball Danes

Great Danes have short coats that are easy to care for, and although they shed a lot, they only need a moderate level of grooming.

The six standard coat colors are Black, Blue, Brindle, Fawn, Harlequin, and Mantle.

Black: When looking for a black Dane, the color should be glossy with no white chest or toe markings.

Blue: Blue Dane puppies are highly prized. Their color varies anywhere from pale gray and charcoal, to slate and deep steel-blue. Their eyes may be amber, dark brown, or, in some cases, pale blue.

Brindle: A brindle coat should ideally be a golden-yellow color with black markings right across the whole body in a chevron shape. The mask, eye rims, ear, and tail tips should also be black.

Fawn: The most common coat color for a Great Dane, also made popular by canine star of the silver screen, Marmaduke. A fawn Dane's coat should be golden yellow, and he should have a defined black muzzle. Ear and tail tips should be black too.

Harlequin: These striking Danes have a white coat with black patches or spots. It is one of the hardest coat colors to perfect and can, therefore, be one of the rarest.

Mantle: These Great Danes appear to have a black blanket thrown over their pure white base coats. While patterns can vary, the most desirable is a pure white muzzle, collar, and front.

From Black to Blue and Harlequin to Mantle, Great Dane coat colors are as impressive and bold as the dogs themselves.

Breed Temperament And Personality Traits

"The Great Dane should be represented as the Apollo of dogs. They should be regal in appearance with a confident but NOT aggressive demeanor. They are passionate about their people and are truly a gentle giant."

Loren Bengston
Glacier Danes

The Great Dane temperament is active yet gentle, which means they are an ideal breed for any busy household with children.

Danes are sensitive souls who need to be trained using positive methods and reinforcement. Harshness can confuse this gentle breed and make them resistant to new ideas and ultimately distrustful.

This breed thrives on human interaction and attention. However, to be happy, Danes crave a lot of attention. They don't do well when they are left to their own devices for hours on end.

Dane owners everywhere lovingly refer to "the zoomies." The zoomies, which seem to come out of nowhere, are a Great Dane's way of releasing all of his excitement and pent-up energy. It's a wild display lasting a couple of minutes whereby the dog leaps or jump over objects, runs frantically in figures of eight, or has short but exuberant bursts of sprinting. You have to see it to believe it!

In a nutshell, think of your Great Dane as your shadow for the next however many years. He will greet you when you arrive home, keep you company in the bathroom, the kitchen, or wherever you happen to be. Plus, he'll want to sleep right next to you every night.

Great Danes will do whatever it takes to be as close to you as they possibly can. A Great Dane, unaware of its physical size, will lean on you, attempt to sit on your lap, and, more often than not, try to watch the TV while resting his vast head on your shoulder.

Great Danes Are Attention Seekers

Danes have no respect for a human's personal space and are 100 percent attention seekers.

Should you deny your Great Dane the love and affection it craves daily, rest assured you will pay the price further on down the line!

Great Danes are bold, brave, and playful. These traits make them ideal for homes with children and even toddlers.

Our second Great Dane, Billy Ray (named by my wife after a famous country-western singer), came to us as a 6-month-old pup. When our daughter was born some three years later, we were naturally concerned about how he would take to the new addition to the family.

Photo Courtesy of Cody & Stephanie Malin

We sought the advice of an animal behaviorist, who advised my wife to gradually take more of a backseat in Billy's life during her pregnancy. He suggested she no longer feed Billy and leave most of his day-to-day care to me. He said when the newborn finally joined our family, Billy wouldn't feel suddenly put aside or rejected.

It was great advice, and when the time came, and our beautiful daughter, Mikki, was born, Billy showed no jealousy whatsoever, only natural curiosity. He seamlessly accepted her into his family and showed her nothing but love and affection.

Right up until the day Billy crossed over to Rainbow Bridge, the only thing bigger than his huge size was his heart.

Is A Great Dane The Right Breed For Your Family?

"They don't do well being kept outside all the time, they really need to live with people. Some Danes are cuddly, some are not, but they all need time with their people."

Barb Bristol
Symmetry Danes

These gentle giants have a heart as huge as their size, and you will be surprised at just how easily a Dane can adapt to living in all sorts of environments.

Pros:
- A Great Dane is content with just one 15-30 minute walk per day
- Danes like nothing more than to spend their time being couch potatoes
- Great Danes are fiercely protective of their families and make excellent watchdogs
- Gentle and tolerant, Danes generally get on well with children of all ages
- A well-trained and socialized Dane who receives sufficient time spent in outdoors can live happily in an apartment
- Although sometimes goofy, Danes are intelligent and eager to please, which makes them relatively easy to train
- Danes usually get on well with other animals
- Their short, thin hair means grooming is at a minimum

Cons:
- A Great Dane's physical size can create a housing challenge, not to mention substantial food bills
- Veterinarian bills can be quite large. Some vets charge for medications based on the weight of their patients!
- Danes are sufficiently tall enough to reach kitchen worktops and can unintentionally knock small children over or injure them

- Danes are the king of drool! So potential Dane owners beware, you will always need to have a towel at the ready to mop up any unwanted slobber!
- On average, a Dane's lifespan is often no more than 6-8 years
- If you intend to take to the road with your canine companion, you will need to invest in a large-size car and a seatbelt!

Only you can answer if a Great Dane is the right dog for you. However, with the right research and a little time spent on getting to know the breed, you're sure to do just fine.

Counting The Costs

In a later chapter, we will take a more in-depth look at the costs of either adopting a Dane from a rescue center or choosing to buy from a breeder.

In the meantime, while you are still deciding on whether this is the dog for you, it's a sensible idea to familiarize yourself with the potential cost of owning a giant breed.

Putting the initial purchase price of your Dane to one side for a moment, be aware that buying a dog of this size is not a small financial responsibility.

Costs can vary depending on how committed you are to your dog's overall ongoing health too.

The big four expenses to initially consider are:

Food

Great Danes may be sturdy in lots of ways, but when it comes to food, they need to follow a careful and strict diet. It's important to make sure your dog gets all the nutrients it needs so ideally its diet should be organic.

Adult dog food needs to be high in fats (minimum of 12%) and proteins (minimum of 23%), and this is especially true in cold weather when your dog needs to build muscle and fat. Commercial dog foods have fat and protein levels that are a lot higher and therefore are not suitable for your dog.

Organic dog foods can be more costly, especially in the vast quantities needed by a dog as huge as a Dane.

With full-grown males weighing between 140 and 180 pounds and females between 110 and 140 pounds, you can imagine just how quickly your bill can mount up.

Puppies are costly too, as to grow up healthily, they need a special diet. What's more, as they grow, so does their appetite. As a rough guide, an adult male Great Dane will eat between 7-10 cups of food a day, which can cost anywhere from $70-$90 per month. Over the space of a year, this can come to as much as $1,000.

Vet Costs

Giant breed dogs can have giant health issues. These include bloat, torsion, hip dysplasia, and cardiomyopathy, a disease of the heart muscle. We will cover these breed-specific issues in depth in a later chapter.

To give you a ballpark figure—an emergency treatment for conditions such as bloat can cost as much as $5,000.For routine veterinary care (excluding the cost of any specialized or emergency treatments), budget for an outlay of $500-$3,000 during the lifetime of your Dane.

Costs are higher than for regular-size dogs since the price for medications and service is more often than not determined by the weight of the dog. This factor is also a consideration for surgeries, procedures, overnight vet clinic stays, and even X-rays.

General Supplies

Remember, your dog is huge! That means everything you need is going to be super-size. Great Dane dogs and puppies need bigger bowls and giant crates and dog beds, as well as sturdier collars and leashes. All this is in addition to large-size bottles of shampoo, more bedding, and of course, you will have to pay a lot more for boarding kennels and daycare.

Is It Worth It?

If you can comfortably afford the cost, then yes, it's worth it! Though Great Danes' large size does bring with it higher bills and a large outlay, they will pay you back tenfold in affection and loyalty.

Doggy Dilemma: Puppy Versus Adult

Once you have decided that a Great Dane is the breed for you, the next dilemma is do you choose a puppy or an adult?

For my family, this has always been the age-old question. During my lifetime, I have been lucky enough to own three Great Danes. The first, Arnold, a 6-year old rescue male with a host of health issues, followed by Billy Ray, a 6-month-old puppy that didn't make the show grade due to his markings. And finally, my family's present and now a senior dog, Jax Teller, purchased as a 10-week-old pup from a reputable breeder.

Adopting a Senior Dog

In Arnold's case, choosing a senior dog was the most rewarding yet heartbreaking decision of our lives. A victim of a marital break-up and no longer manageable for his single owner, Arnold had a lot of health and separation issues.

With his owner unable to afford either the volume or quality of food needed to keep him healthy, Arnold's health had gone into rapid decline. By the time he joined our family, he weighed less than 50 pounds.

We knew what we were taking on when we adopted him from the rescue center. And even though his time with us was relatively short, I can honestly say I have never known such affection from a dog in such a short space of time. He gave so much love in return and left a huge hole in all our hearts when he finally passed.

In our case, we were lucky; Arnold was fully housetrained, well socialized, and he settled with us almost immediately. It was as if he knew he had a second chance, and he clung on to life with all four of his big paws.

So my best advice is, before you make straight for the puppy pen, have a good, long hard think about giving a mature Dane a home and consider the basic pros and cons.

Pros:
- Rewarding experience
- Less initial cost than adopting a puppy from a breeder
- Animals are already vaccinated and should have received a full health check
- Your adoptive dog may already be housetrained

Cons:
- Existing health conditions
- Danes have a short life span so you will have less time with them
- An unsocialized adult may be more difficult to train
- Potential behavioral issues

Adopting an Adolescent

After Arnold came Billy Ray—a rambunctious crazy boy who, having lived in a kennel, albeit a luxurious one for all his young life, had very few social skills.

He came from a reputable breeder and had been bred for show purposes, and his family members were a long line of Cruft's winners. The breeder knew he didn't have what it would take to become a champion but couldn't bear to part with him, so at 6 months old, his adoption options were limited.

Our veterinarian, having been there every step of the way with our first Great Dane Arnold, suggested to the breeder she meet with us and see if we were a good fit for him.

I remember him bounding up to my five-foot-two father-in-law, jumping on his lap, and planting a big muddy paw print right in the middle of his forehead.

Danes grow really quickly, and the beauty of adopting an adolescent is you get a good insight into the size of the huge dog you will be sharing your home with.

Adolescent Danes are like teenage kids. They think they know better and want to be the leader of the pack, which in Billy's case was me, our 5-year-old female Chihuahua, and a 3-year-old male cross-breed. It didn't take very long for the Chihuahua to lick Billy into shape though, and within a few weeks, he was no longer acting out. The thing about Great Danes is, they are intelligent and generally quick to learn, so even though we were starting training a little late in the day, we got there in the end.

By the time Billy crossed over Rainbow Bridge at age 6, he had proved himself a loyal dog to me, a protector to my wife and daughter, and the best dog ever.

Billy will always be a champion to us.

When you are adopting an adolescent, the same pros and cons apply as for senior dogs. However, you have to also consider why an adolescent dog is being offered for adoption.

Danes grow really quickly, and the beauty of adopting an adolescent is you get a good insight into the size of the huge dog you will be sharing your home with.

Adopting a Puppy

Great Dane puppies are all big ears and baggy skin, and like all small things, they are ridiculously adorable.

Puppies are a blank canvas, which means you have to teach them everything they need to know from day one. Given the right training and socialization, a puppy will grow into a well-adjusted adult dog.

A cute puppy now, but an untrained giant dog in the years to come, is sure to be a huge problem for everyone.

Remember too, the size of the accident is relative to the size of the puppy! The same goes for temper tantrums, chewing, digging holes, and everything in between.

As they grow and become more inquisitive, Danes will counter-surf, meaning you need to keep everything out of reach. Not only do you not want dinner drooled all over, but you also don't need a huge vet bill for a dog who has woofed down a poisonous cleaning product.

Even at a very young age, a Dane puppy can do a lot of damage to your belongings, to your home, and especially to your outside space.

So if you are a particularly neat and tidy person who likes everything in its place, this giant breed might be one to reconsider.

Great Danes are not yard dogs. They don't like to be left alone for long periods of a time, and puppies in particular need as much human contact as you can give them.

We adopted our current senior Dane, Jax Teller, as a puppy from a well-known breeder. We were with him 24/7 in the very beginning and have subsequently reaped the rewards. Yes, he made mistakes at the outset but then so did we. However, these were few and far between so for some, it's a great idea to adopt a Great Dane puppy, provided you are prepared to put the time and effort into training, of course.

CHAPTER 2
Choosing Your Great Dane

Rescue Center Versus Breeder

"I would research the breeder and ask to look at their premises. There are many breeders who will not allow families on their premises which should be a red flag. Anyone looking to add a Dane should be allowed to look at not only the conditions the dogs are living in but also look at the dogs and interact with them. If you are adopting from a rescue then ask questions. Find out why the dog was given to the rescue. Most rescues are very open and honest about any dog that was surrendered. If a rescue can't answer your questions then I would look elsewhere."

Shawna Howard
Cottonball Danes

Photo Courtesy of Sarah Wagner

Photo Courtesy of
Sonia West

Whether you are adopting a Great Dane puppy from a breeder or an adult dog from a Great Dane rescue center, the choice is yours. There are lots of Dane breeders and a growing number of Great Dane rescue centers are offering more of this breed for adoption.

Having gone down both routes with success, I've gathered some useful information to help guide you through the decision-making process.

The best way to explore both options is to compare one with the other. Don't assume that just because a dog is in a shelter, it is either badly behaved or sick. From divorce to redundancy, there are many reasons why a family pet may have been unfortunate enough to find themselves homeless.

Looking for a Fresh Start

The majority of Danes in a rescue center will be adult dogs looking for a fresh start. The plus side of rescuing one of these gentle giants, apart from the obvious feel-good factor, is that you may well get a fully housetrained, socialized adult dog.

Be aware, though, that the average life span of a Great Dane is short. So prepare yourself for the fact that your adoptive Dane might not be with you for as many years as you would like.

In a lot of cases, the rescue center will have some information as to the background of the dog and may be aware of any underlying health issues.

Photo Courtesy of
Brittney Anderson

If they don't, you could be offering a home to a dog with existing behavioral issues. Fear can trigger a mild to severe reaction, ranging from hiding or trembling to a total loss of control and even result in them harming themselves or others. The cause of this could be something as simple as a thunderstorm, a noise, a smell, etc., or, as I discovered with a Cane Corso I once fostered, pickup trucks.

One rescue Great Dane I know of was terrified of fire. Juno, a 4-year-old Harlequin, was adopted by a friend of mine, and all was well for a long time. Until one day, my friend lit a bonfire in his garden.

Juno was terrified when he saw the flames, and so we can only assume that somewhere in his past, he had a bad experience with fire, and the bonfire had triggered his memory.

It took a little while to get Juno back on track, but with lots of patience and understanding, he is now overcoming his fear.

Love at First Sight

When my family adopted Arnold from a rescue center, we knew very well that he had health issues. He was very underweight and lethargic, his coat was poor, and his eyes gave the game away—he was giving up.

Out of all the Great Danes available for adoption, for my wife, it was love at first sight.

So we decided to offer him a loving home for the remainder of his life.

We had the funds to cover any medical costs and the one-on-one time to give to him. We had a tough time persuading the rescue center to let us adopt him but agreed to keep them fully in the loop about his progress.

It isn't something that we will ever regret, but taking on an adult dog of any breed requires love and endless patience. Remember, this is never more so than in the case of a 110-plus-pound dog.

On the flip side, when you buy a puppy from a breeder, you leave less to luck. Plus, of course, you can choose what color coat you want your dog to have. You will be made aware of the puppy's genetics, and very often get to see its parents and siblings.

I will go into more depth about how to choose a breeder further on in this chapter.

Rescue Center Research

"For families seeking to rescue a Great Dane, I think they need to be honest about their experience in canine behavior modification and general training. It is often the case that Great Danes in rescue organizations possess bad habits that, coupled with their large size makes for a difficult task. Though many will expect a rescued Great Dane to present their goofy and loving side with ease, the change in homes can present unforeseen challenges. Therefore, if it is indeed a rescue dog a family is seeking, being honest about the level of training they can commit to from the first day is vital to living a peaceful life with their new dog."

Nathan Bolby
Grand Mimeux

With the number of homeless dogs looking for forever homes higher than ever before, never has it been more important for potential dog owners to consider rescuing rather than buying their future pet.

Once you have decided that re-homing a Dane from a rescue center is something you would like to explore, the next burning question is how to begin your research.

The only way to do this research is through time and effort, and like most things in this day and age, your first point of call is the internet.

Visit as many sites as you can. Some centers may not be located close to where you live but could have a large coverage area. If they don't, then you will need to decide how far you are willing to travel to find your furry friend. You don't want to fall in love with a photo of your perfect pet, only to discover that the center is thousands of miles away.

Once you have made this decision, the next step is to make a list of the Great Dane Rescue Centers that are within your traveling range.

Read everything each site has to say, and don't skip straight to the photo gallery.

Look for the center's terms and conditions and privacy policy. Also, is there a testimonial section where previous adopters have recommended the center?

Does the center have a Facebook page or blog? Here, you can chat with current owners and discover some of the ups and downs of rescue Great Dane ownership.

Some Great Dane rescue centers have special events you can get involved in, and may even offer advice on financial assistance for pets.

It's a good idea if you can, to visit as many centers as possible and see which one has the feel-good factor. If this isn't possible, talk to them on the phone or email them with any questions or concerns.

HELPFUL TIP
Research the Breed

According to the Great Dane Club of America (gdca.org) and Great Dane Rescue (greatdaneres-cueinc.com), adoption is a viable alternative to purchasing a Great Dane puppy. Adult dogs have proven traits and characteristics. Any negative behaviors can be observed in adult dogs before welcoming them into your home.

Finally, contact your local veterinarian and find out if the practice has any Great Dane Rescue Center contacts, or even contact a vet in the area of the center you are considering adopting from. They may have local knowledge or advice to help you make your decision.

Re-homing a Dog Is a Serious Business

Don't hurry the process; this is a big breed, and it's an even bigger decision to offer an adult Dane a home.

Re-homing an adult Great Dane is a serious business. Whereas a puppy is a blank canvas, an adult dog's personality has already been formed by its previous owner(s). Don't discard adult or senior dogs, though. "You can't teach an old dog new tricks" simply isn't true. With love, trust, and guidance, a dog can learn at any age. You will, however, need to have patience when choosing an adult Dane from a rescue center.

The center will hopefully have information about his previous family, the reasons for the dog's abandonment, and a good idea of its temperament and behavior around others.

You will also need to find out about any previous or ongoing health issues and medications.

You can begin by asking a kennel worker to walk the dog on a leash. In doing this, you can find out if the dog is happy to venture out from the security of its kennel or if it has to be encouraged. A dog that walks well on the leash has, in all probability, had some training in other areas too.

Remember that a shelter dog may be overexcited to venture back out into the big wide world, so don't be put off if he initially pulls on the leash or is over exuberant. Give the dog time to settle down before judging its behavior.

A dog's body language is the key to understanding its state of mind. A fearful dog will have its ears pulled back, tail tucked (if not docked), and its body low to the ground. Ideally, a relaxed dog will have a loose posture and stand upright. If you have young children or elderly people in your home, you also don't want a 100-plus-pound dog that jumps up at every opportunity, so watch out for this.

Take a dog treat with you and ask the kennel worker if it's okay to offer it to the dog. It should be interested but not aggressive. If you put the snack on the ground, can you approach the dog without any growling? A Great Dane with food aggression issues is not for the faint-hearted.

If you know anyone with lots of large-dog experience, take them with you. Perhaps they can give you an objective opinion on whether or not the dog will be hard to train. It's even worth paying a professional dog trainer to go along with you. It can save a lot of heartache in the long run.

When you come to an informed decision as to which dog you want to offer a home to, remember to give it a few months rather than days or weeks to adapt to its new life.

Photo Courtesy of Tamasin Pocock Tamzdane Great Danes

Finding A Breeder

"The breeder should encourage the buyer to come to their home, meet the Danes they own, interact with the puppies. All puppies should be well socialized, clean and vaccinated at the time of placement."

Carolyn McNamara
Divine Acres Great Danes

You don't just want to find any Great Dane breeder; you want to find a *great* one!

If all things go well, your new puppy will hopefully be with you for many years, so this is a very important step in the process.

Although buying a puppy from a breeder rather than adopting an adult Dane from a rescue center doesn't 100% guarantee a healthy dog, the odds are definitely in your favor.

To this end, the Great Dane Club of America (GDCA) has an ethical code for Great Dane breeders to follow. It gives guidelines not only for ethical breeding but also for responsible ownership.

Again, this is not a process you can hurry.

Finding a breeder is very like researching a rescue center. First, decide on the distance you are willing to travel to find your canine companion.

Check out the list of breeders on the GDCA site. It is conveniently organized by state.

You can also surf the internet and make a list of Great Dane breeders within your chosen area. Remember, many will specialize in specific coat colors, so if you have set your heart on a particular coat variation, you will need to make sure that the breeder you research has upcoming litters available in this choice.

Make sure your research includes:

- Viewing recent photos of their kennels and facilities—does it look clean?
- Checking out photos of their sires and dams

- Reading owner testimonials. Find out if it's possible to get in touch with previous owners. Can you chat with them and find out about the temperament and health of their puppy?
- Asking to speak with the breeder's veterinarian
- Visits to the various breeders who eventually make your short-list

Don't be afraid to ask questions. Any reputable breeder will see this as a good sign that you will be a responsible owner. So pass on any that don't!

Photo Courtesy of Nikki Lynn

What To Expect From A Breeder

"A breeder should readily have available pedigrees, quality pictures of their dogs showing structure, as well as results from OFA/Pennhip health testing. They should welcome families into their homes after interviewing, and their dogs and puppies should be raised in clean safe environments and fed a quality diet."

Carrie Michaelson
Gem Danes

Here are some questions to raise that will help you ensure you're buying from a reputable breeder:

- How long have you been breeding Great Danes, and what is your breed experience?
- Do your Danes live inside or out? There is no right answer to this, but it does give you an insight into potential socialization
- Can you introduce me to either or both of my potential puppy's parents?
- What health tests have the parents undergone to rubber stamp that they have no genetic diseases specific to the Great Dane breed?
- Are you happy for me to talk to past buyers and your veterinarian?
- Do puppies have a record of up-to-date vaccinations and can you provide a health guarantee along with the contract? If so, what does the guarantee cover, and for how long does it run?
- How do you socialize your puppies, and will you be giving me written info on how to care for my pup?
- Should something go wrong, is there a return policy in place?
- What happens to your dogs that become too old to breed? Some breeders euthanize their dogs that can no longer reproduce, and the answer to this question can tell you a lot about the breeder
- Are you available to talk to, and can you offer advice and support throughout the lifetime of my Great Dane?

Breeders should be caring, willing to share advice and information, and knowledgeable about the Great Dane breed. Once an agreement has been made the breeder will give you, as the adopter, a contract to sign. The content of this contract will vary from breeder to breeder. Some will offer simple contracts while others may be a lot more comprehensive.

In all probability it will include the breeder's terms, the buyer's responsibility, and a health guarantee.

It is important to read through the document very carefully and make sure you understand what you are agreeing to.

Don't be afraid to take the contract home with you to fully digest it, or to maybe ask someone knowledgeable to read it over for you.

Choosing The Right Pup Or Dog

First off, check that your rescue center or breeder can provide the necessary paperwork to confirm that all future pets have undergone full veterinary examinations. They should have treatment for worms and other parasites and their vaccinations up-to-date before re-homing or adoption.

Once you have established this, the next thing to do is choose the right pet for you.

When choosing a puppy from a breeder, you can look out for a number of important things.

A healthy puppy should be alert and not lethargic. Take a small toy with you when you visit the breeder and play with the pup. When you toss a toy, the pup's eye should follow its path. It's also an excellent way to check that it runs and jumps normally too.

Clap your hands and see if the puppy responds. Puppies should be interested in people and play nicely around their littermates. A scared puppy that wets itself out of fear may be more challenging to train. Conversely, a puppy that plays nicely with its brothers and sisters, and backs off when one of its littermates yelps, will in all probability socialize well with other dogs.

Touch the puppy's, ears, and paws. Very gently roll him onto his back. This test is an excellent way to see whether your puppy has any aggressive tendencies or is well adjusted. A happy puppy should act relaxed and submissive.

Once you have established which puppy has the best personality for you, make sure that its coat is healthy with no dry or bald patches. Check that its ears, eyes, and nose are clean and free from any discharge.

It should breathe easily with no signs of coughing or sneezing.

These are all simple things that can be carried out on a brief visit and are a good indication of the mental and physical state of your new addition.

Is Two Company?

Great Danes are a sociable breed and need constant companionship. They don't do well when they are left alone for long periods, and so for me, two is definitely company.

Dogs are primarily pack animals, and for my family, it has solved the problem of my Danes getting lonely when we have to leave the house. I do know, however, for some, it has meant twice as much hard work.

A naughty dog can lead its playmate astray. They can teach one another bad tricks and habits, and two can undoubtedly do a lot more damage than one!

On the plus side, two dogs can keep each other entertained, leaving you to get on with whatever you have to do, whether at home or work. They are less likely to be stressed or anxious as they can rely on each other for companionship.

Double Trouble!

If you get two puppies at the same time, then it's potentially double trouble, so be prepared! It's not all bad news though; puppies can learn good habits from one another as well as bad, so are often easier to train.

For me, the secret of success comes down to establishing the pack leader.

If you decide to bring home a second dog and you already have an existing dog, then don't leave them alone until you know they get along well with each other. The newer addition may, depending on its age and gender, challenge the first dog, and this can result in a vet bill.

It is vital to set the rules from the outset and establish that you, as the owner, are the pack leader. Once you establish this, things will settle down, and natural order will follow.

Sharing a home with two dogs can be rewarding, but it does, of course, double the feeding and vet costs, not to mention the care and cleaning up!

CHAPTER 3
Preparing For Your New Arrival

Preparing Your Home For Your New Great Dane

"New owners should take a look at their floor coverings. A growing Great Dane needs traction in order for the paw, muscles, and bones to work and form correctly. If they are kept on slippery surfaces during their developmental time, issues of the joints can develop. Laying down area rugs is a great solution to this problem."

Nathan Bolby
Grand Mimeux

Photo Courtesy of
Nikki Lynn

Photo Courtesy of
Taylor Cook

Before you welcome your Great Dane to its new home, it's important to not only gather the necessary supplies, but to prepare your house so it's safe and comfortable for your new arrival.

Supplies You'll Need include:

- Food and Bowls
- Dog Bed, Bedding, and Crate
- Grooming Tools
- Toys

- Collars and Leashes
- Coats
- First Aid Kit

Food And Bowls

For puppies: Ask your breeder to advise you on the best possible food for your puppy.

Great Dane puppies cannot be fed regular dog food because it usually has too high a protein level and Dane puppies must not have foods that promote fast growth. Stock up on the food you will need for the first few weeks. Remember, your new puppy will need to eat at least three times a day. Eating only once a day can increase your puppy's chances of fatal bloat.

For adult dogs: Ask the rescue center to advise you on the best possible food for your dog.

Your dog may have special dietary needs, and changing its diet may cause unnecessary health problems. When you rescue a dog, it's natural to want to spoil it, but this isn't always in the dog's best interest. Personally, when adopting any rescue dog, I have always asked if I could buy food from the shelter and gently weaned my dog onto a better quality brand. Adult dogs will also need a raised feeding and water bowl; this can help prevent bloat.

Dog Beds, Bedding, And Crates

TOP TIP

If you have the space, you can't go wrong if you invest in a child's extendable bed with metal frame and wooden slats. They may cost more at the outset, but ours (from a certain Swedish flat-pack furniture store) has taken us from pup to senior and lasted for many, many years. They are easy to keep clean and smell less doggy! Plus, you can replace the thin mattress element as needed rather than purchasing a whole new dog bed.

Make sure that dog beds are robust and large enough to accommodate the weight of your dog. You may even have to order the correct size from your pet store, as many will not have them in stock.

Adult Great Danes will get pressure sores from sleeping on hard surfaces, and so ideally, beds should be raised.

You will also need lots of comfy bedding so make sure you have a good supply of blankets and towels on hand.

It's always a good idea to invest in a suitable size crate that will accommodate your Great Dane from puppy to adult.

Grooming Tools

Grooming a Dane is low maintenance.

So start by going to your local pet store and buying a basic grooming kit. This kit should include:

- A good quality brush
- Nail clippers
- Shampoo
- Pet ear wipes
- Toothbrush and toothpaste

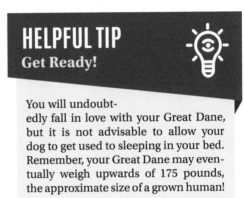

HELPFUL TIP

Get Ready!

You will undoubtedly fall in love with your Great Dane, but it is not advisable to allow your dog to get used to sleeping in your bed. Remember, your Great Dane may eventually weigh upwards of 175 pounds, the approximate size of a grown human!

Toys

Keep your new puppy busy with lots and lots of sturdy chew toys. The same goes for adult dogs—but only when you are sure they have no guarding issues. The same goes for snacks. Your rescue center may be able to advise you on this.

Collars And Leashes

Measure your puppy or dog and make sure you get a correctly fitting collar and a leash suitable for your new dog's weight and size. Avoid retractable leads.

TOP TIP

Look into purchasing a doggy seat belt too. An adult dog hitting you on the back of the head or lurching into the front seat is a force to be reckoned with.

Coats

Great Danes are susceptible to harsh weather conditions, so you may want to invest in a warm and waterproof coat for your gentle giant.

First Aid Kit

Buy a first aid kit in your local vet practice, pet store, or make up your own. Whatever you do, make sure you have one handy. Apart from the usual bandages and antiseptic cream, ask your vet about a bloat kit. Should bloat occur, time is of the essence, and this could mean the difference between life and death for your Dane (you can learn more about bloat in Chapter 6).

Better to be safe than sorry, and as the Scouts say, Be Prepared!

Photo Courtesy of
Cassandra Perez

Eliminating Potential Home Hazards

"It's so important to make sure, especially if you have children, to pick up toys the dog is not allowed to have. Dog toys should be large enough they can't be swallowed and any chews should be digestible."

Carrie Michaelson
Gem Danes

Whether an adult or puppy, your new addition is bound to get into some sort of trouble. By eliminating any potential hazards before you bring the pup home, you can minimize the problems.

Potential indoor hazards can be avoided by:

- Removing any breakable or valuable objects. You don't want that long whippy tail to hit your flat-screen TV!

- Cable tying loose wires throughout the house

- Moving your kids' favorite toys to a safe place and putting away any others with small pieces that could choke a puppy

- If you have expensive rugs, you may want to temporarily remove them while you housetrain your pet

- Considering non-slip matting for shiny floors

- If you are adopting an adult Dane, clearing all kitchen work surfaces of cleaning products and food is essential. You will soon become familiar with the term "counter surfing." Everyday foods we humans love, including grapes, chocolate, and nuts, are highly toxic for dogs. So keep food in high cupboards or sealed containers and cleaning/laundry products well out of reach

- Making sure that dish towels and laundry aren't left lying around (just before Christmas one year, I got a $1,500 vet bill because my Great Dane ate a dish towel and three pairs of socks. This meal resulted in us having to cancel our vacation to Spain!)

- Installing child or doggy gates where necessary

- Storing all medication, animal or human, in a locked medicine cabinet

- Keeping the toilet seat closed at all times

Photo Courtesy of
Chloe Shaw

Creating A Safe Space Outdoors

While Great Danes don't need a lot of room and lots live indoors all day, they do need regular daily exercise. They can live outside too in a secure and suitable place but can't be deprived of human company.

The first thing to be aware of when offering a Great Dane a home is, forget having a neat and tidy garden or a perfect lawn.

Think of your dog as a small pony who literally churns up the mud, grass, and anything under its huge paws as it gallops around the outside space.

So if gardening is your thing, your first job is to fence off a dog-friendly space where your Dane can get the zoomies without you tearing your hair out.

Here are a few more hints and tips of what you can do to make your outside space safe and fun.

- Check that the plants in your garden aren't toxic and fence off or remove any that are. There are gardening books available on this subject but common toxic plants include Aconitum, Amaryllis, Asparagus Fern, Azalea, Cyclamen, Daffodil bulbs, Delphiniums, Foxgloves, Hemlock, Hyacinth, Hydrangea, Ivy, Laburnum, Lily of the Valley, Lupins, Morning glory, Nightshade, Oleander, Rhododendron, Rhubarb leaves, Sweet Peas, Tulip bulbs, Umbrella plant, Wisteria and Yew.
- Walk the perimeter of your yard or garden and check for any holes or gaps in fencing.
- Deter your Dane from digging up plants by scattering the soil around with spices such as dried pepper or mustard. Rosemary, bitter orange, and sage work well too
- Securing your back yard, front yard, and any other yard space, making sure there are no gaps in the fencing
- Making sure that swimming pools along with any hot tubs are either inaccessible or covered
- If your dog has access to your shed or garage, make sure that any chemicals, pesticides, poisons, cleaning products, antifreeze, etc., are out of reach
- Great Danes don't jump, or so I was once told. Wrong! Some do, mine once cleared a 5-foot farm gate. So make sure that fencing and gates

Photo Courtesy of Elizabeh Logue

are a suitable height. Fencing should also be sturdy enough to withstand a jumping 100-plus-pound dog

- If your gentle giant is going to be outside for long periods of time, provide a sun, wind, and waterproof shelter
- Some dogs enjoy pulling up flowers, so fence off your prize-winning roses
- Make sure all garden implements are safely stowed away, including hoses! The same goes for fertilizers, rat poison, and weed killer, etc.
- Garbage bins need to have secure lids or be inaccessible
- Be aware bark chips are poisonous to dogs
- Outdoor hot tubs, ponds, and swimming pools should be fenced off or securely covered
- Securely lock garages, outbuildings, and sheds

Whatever the breed or size of your new dog, making the outside space safe is crucial. Remember though, that until you get to know your pouch, never leave them outside alone.

Preparing Your Children For The Great Dane

A Great Dane is the most gentle of all giant breeds. They are playful, affectionate, and protective, which makes them the perfect companion for you and young members of your family.

However, their giant stature means they can accidentally hurt a small child.

Welcoming a puppy or adult Dane into your family is a cause for great excitement, but you should also approach it with some degree of caution.

Children can play hard. They can kick, shout, scream, and be rowdy. Fortunately, you have chosen one of the most patient breeds of dogs on the planet. They are intelligent enough to understand the difference between rough play and aggression and, as such, will put up with an awful lot.

I have never allowed a dog to play with younger children unsupervised, and I would certainly not recommend it for anyone adopting an adult dog.

If you are raising a puppy, then you can be a little less cautious, but again, supervision is needed with toddlers and young children. A swipe of the tail can cause a lot of pain, as can one of those giant paws standing on a small foot or hand. Even a non-aggressive bite when playing can hurt tiny fingers.

TOP TIP

- Create a safe space for your pet, such as a dog crate, where it can get a well-earned break from the craziness, and explain to your child that the dog must stay in the crate until you say it is okay to let it out.
Teach children from a very early age to respect animals, and you will minimize any future problems.
- Explain to your child regardless of their age that a new puppy brings responsibility and it is not acceptable to hit, kick, smack, hurt, or tease any animal.
- Make children fully aware that they must be careful around the new puppy at mealtimes and not touch their food or bowls while they are eating.
- Very young children need to be warned that a puppy is not a toy and should not be treated like one.
- Depending on the age of your child, give your child some level of responsibility. This could range from brushing the puppy to making sure its area is cozy for bedtime.

CHAPTER 4
Welcoming Your Great Dane Home

"They have an immense love for their people. Once a Dane makes a friend of you, you have a friend for life. They are giants with a heart to match."

Jackie Herman
Ace-Hi DanesBringing Your Great Dane Home

Photo Courtesy of Andrea Albrecht

Once you've picked up your dog either from the breeder or rescue, it's time to safely transport him home.

It's a good idea to gather a few items for the all-important journey. What you need will depend on the length of the journey and of course, whether you have adopted a puppy or a dog.

These items could include:

- Water and food bowls
- Bottled water
- Food
- A blanket and a towel
- Wet wipes
- Healthy chews
- Pet pads and newspapers along with some kitchen paper towels
- Collar and leash
- Plastic trash bags for waste
- Anti-bacterial hand gel

HELPFUL TIP
Investing in Your Great Dane

The initial cost of adopting a Great Dane is approximately $400, while purchasing a puppy from a breeder may reach $3,000. Although this preliminary cost can be expected, other costs such as food and veterinary care are often overlooked and not anticipated. Expect food costs to be about $60-$100 per month for your Great Dane.

Remember, until a puppy has had all of its vaccinations you shouldn't take it out for walks in public places, but you can carry them.

If you have just adopted a cute puppy, you may want to hold him on your lap on the way home, but this is absolutely inadvisable. Whenever you travel with your Great Dane in the car, he must always be restrained. If you have to brake suddenly, your un-crated or un-tethered pet could go flying through the windshield. Or, he could cause an accident by climbing into the front to be with you.

Your Great Dane, puppy or adult, depending on the duration of the journey, will need to take a toilet break. As a rule of thumb, a 10- to 12-week-old puppy will need to relieve itself every 2-3 hours. If you stop on the road, you will need to put a clean puppy pad on the floor or newspaper for the little one to stand on.

An adult dog may be able to hold for 5-6 hours.

In both cases though, remember your new pet will be nervous or over-excited, so it's a good idea to make a pit stop every couple of hours.

Photo Courtesy of Cassie Heidmann

Avoid feeding your Great Dane if possible on or before the journey as this may lead to travel sickness. If your dog is about to vomit it may begin to excessively drool and become subdued.

Dog Guards

This custom made or universal-fit partition attaches across the width of the rear seats, creating a secure area in the back of the car. If you've got something like a station wagon or an SUV with a tailgate, this is ideal.

It creates a safe space for your Great Dane and as they're generally good travelers, you don't need to tell them twice to jump in when they see that tailgate open. Just make sure the dog is not too cramped and can see out the windows.

The partition also works even if you don't have a rear cargo area. All you have to do is use elasticized tie downs or bungee cords to attach the partition to the rear of the front seat headrests.

Safety Restraints

Using a seat belt or strap is another possibility for keeping your new dog safe in the car both today and on all future journeys. Just make sure you don't attach a securing belt or strap to your dog's collar. Instead, you'll need a good-quality secure harness fitted around the dog's chest and back. To this, you will need to attach your leash to the harness' D-ring.

A belt buckle clip with an enclosed anchoring point clicks into the lower female section of the seat belt buckle to which you attach the other end of the leash.

Don't Send Your Dog into Sensory Overload!

Last but not least, a couple of real obvious points that a new owner may overlook. Firstly, your Great Dane has around 300 million scent receptors in their nose and sticking their head out of the car window can send them into sensory overload.

While their jowl-wobbling, ear-flapping antics may be highly entertaining to other road users, it's potentially dangerous to the dog and best not to encourage it from day one.

Secondly, and of real importance, never leave your Dane (or any animal for that matter) in a vehicle that's going to get too hot or too cold. Apart from possibly causing mental and physical pain and stress, you could also be breaking the law.

Arriving Home

Photo Courtesy of Brianne Turpin

Ask your family members to stand back as you bring the dog into the house. Guide the dog into a designated and secure space. Keep things calm and let your Dane get used to his space. Show your Great Dane his crate or bed and water bowl. Give him space in this restricted area while he settles in, and keep stimulation to a minimum.

Once the dog is relaxed, gradually let your family meet him, one at a time. If your Great Dane is nervous or backs away, so should they.

Every 2-3 hours, put the dog on a leash and take it for a potty break. Do this even if you have a garden or yard. If you have to leave the animal for a short time or its bedtime, put him in the crate or bed.

Start as you mean to go on. If you don't intend your puppy or dog to sleep in your bedroom with you, then don't cave in and bring his bed in with you on the first night!

Creating A Schedule

Creating and sticking to a routine or schedule is important for you and your new family pet, regardless of whether it's a puppy or adult dog.

A set schedule not only shows your new pet what is expected of him but also what he can expect from you.

Although your Dane will need to fit in around your family commitments, here is an idea of what your dog's schedule ideally should look like.

Pre-Breakfast: Time to wake up and go out. Take your puppy or dog outside to relieve himself. It's also a good time to play with your pup or bond with your adult dog.

Breakfast: Feed your Dane and give him lots of fresh water. To reduce the odds of bloat you should always wait at least 60 minutes before or after exercise to feed your dog.

Post-Breakfast: Take your dog for a walk or go out into the yard or garden and check that he has done his business. Even if it's raining, don't leave your new Dane to his own devices.

Mid-Morning: If you are at home, now is a great time to bond with your dog. Puppies will probably nap while an adult dog will be happy to hang out with you while you work. For a rescue dog, the days before coming home to you have probably been boring, with little or no stimulation, so take your time and don't overload his senses.

Noon: Lunchtime for pups followed by a potty trip outside. For adults, play time outside under your supervision. To reduce the odds of bloat, remember again to wait for at least 60 minutes before or after exercise to feed your dog.

Mid-Day: Play followed by a potty break and a nap for pups. Chill out time for adult dogs.

Dinner Time: Time for dinner for both adults and pups, again followed by a potty trip or walk outside at least 60 minutes after eating.

Evening: Wear your puppy out with lots of play, and make sure he burns off all his energy before bedtime. A walk is also a good idea at this time or even a run around the yard. A puppy should always have a potty break after playtime regardless of the time of day. For adults, the evening is a good time to get your dog used to the family. Sit down and watch TV, read a book, and let your dog start to get used to his new life. Remember to take him outside. A rescue dog may be used to relieving himself in his kennel and may not be housetrained. Patience is the key here.

Bedtime: Your new Great Dane needs a set bedtime and this must fit in with your needs. Whether that's 8 p.m. or 1 a.m., make sure it becomes routine. Whatever time you decide upon, take your Dane for one last trip outside before bed. Settle your pup or dog down for the night in his crate or bed and say goodnight.

Your Dane will adapt to his new environment a lot faster if you set a schedule, and as far as is humanly possible, stick to it on a daily basis.

First Week Expectations

"The first few weeks are always a transition period for your puppy. They are adjusting to new smells, people, sounds, and environments. If you are house training, then be prepared for accidents. Everything is new, just remember to be patient!"

Shawna Howard
Cottonball Danes

You will need to be patient and give your dog time to adjust to his new environment.

While pups are naturally trusting and embrace new experiences, an adult dog from a rescue center may be wary. It could take a few months rather than a couple of weeks for him to feel safe and comfortable.

Every case is different and every Dane unique, but taking time out and getting to know your dog during the first week is critical.

With **Day 1** under your belt (as discussed earlier), **Day 2** is about getting to know one another. Allow your Dane to come to you. The best place to do this is in his designated area. It's not too early to work on a few basic tricks such as "sit" and "fetch," as this can help you both to bond. Reward your dog with a healthy treat and lots of verbal praise.

It's early days, so if you take a rescue dog for a walk, try and make it somewhere quiet where you are unlikely to come into contact with heavy traffic, people, or animals. Also, puppies that have not been fully vaccinated should not be exposed to other animals, or be allowed to walk on public areas.

By **Day 3,** you can allow your Great Dane into your living area for short bursts of time. With your dog on a leash, allow him to explore a few areas of your home. Take your Dane out for a walk and continue to build trust.

When **Day 4** dawns, it's time to give your Great Dane a taste of normal life. Allow your dog to have more time out of his designated area. Still keep access to other areas of the home to a minimum, but start to allow your dog more freedom.

Hopefully, by **Day 5** your dog is ready to become part of the family. He should be ready to spend time with your family in general areas of your home. Keep a watchful eye on how your dog responds to other pets and family members and see if he displays any dominance or guarding behaviors.

Continue with routine walks outside the house and try to slowly introduce your Dane to other dogs and humans.

With **Day 6 and 7** comes more freedom, inside the house and out. You will still need, however, to crate or put your dog in his designated place when you are out of the home.

While puppies need patience, if you are working with a rescue dog, you also need an open mind. Obstacles will come up from time to time, so don't be disappointed when things don't go according to plan.

Additional Tips

Some people will tell you that when you first take your Great Dane outside the house, you should keep it on a leash for the first 7-14 days. I would suggest that until you know your adult rescue Dane inside and out, extend this period indefinitely.

It's not only important to understand how your dog interacts with others, human and four-legged, but you also need to be confident that you can recall your Great Dane when needed. So spend time and get to know your dog before you let him run free in the outside world.

You can expect your new family member to want to explore his living space, so keep all doors closed and don't allow him to free-roam around the house. My family's open-door policy once resulted in muddy paw prints on freshly washed sheets and a nest built out of white fluffy towels!

During the first week or so, there will be accidents, and depending on whether you have opted for a puppy or adult, these may be sizeable! So take the time to go outside with your Great Dane when he takes a potty break. All of our Danes (young and old) have hated the rain, and unless my daughter stood there with a golf umbrella over her and their heads, they just wouldn't go!

Believe me, you will reap what you sow! Time and effort put in during these early days will result in you having a truly amazing experience with this Apollo of dogs.

Photo Courtesy of
Jessica Woolley

Getting Through the First Few Weeks

Your puppy has arrived, and that big ball of baggy skin is now 2-3 months old and growing in size and independence daily. He is gaining in confidence and soaking up new information like a veritable sponge.

The first few weeks of puppy ownership are vital because during this time, it is important that you make your puppy's experiences good ones. Negative experiences can leave an everlasting impression on your new puppy.

This period is the time to lay the foundations of what will be a happy, healthy, and long relationship.

- Spend as much time as possible with your new arrival. Your Great Dane puppy shouldn't be left alone for long periods of time.
- Encourage appropriate forms of play. You must teach your puppy not to bite, so make sure you always have a good selection of dog toys on hand.
- Keep the handling of your puppy by visitors to a minimum. If a child unintentionally hurts your dog by being too rough or dropping him, it can affect your dog's perception of other humans.
- Pay attention to how your puppy is adjusting to his new surroundings. A good sign that a puppy feels secure is a wagging tail!

Once your puppy is fully vaccinated and able to interact in the outside world, now is a great time to think about enrolling in training classes.

Introducing Your Great Dane To Existing Pets

In general, Great Danes are friendly toward other dogs. But what if you're bringing a Dane into a house with existing pets?

The answer to this depends on the family pet in question.

Danes have a natural curiosity, and this, together with having no impression of their physical size, can sometimes be an issue. Depending on just how protective of their territory they are, your existing pet can also affect the outcome.

Dogs

Here, first impressions count and, to some extent, will form the basis for future relationships. While some owners believe it's a good idea to put both dogs in the yard and let them sort things out between themselves, in my opinion, it isn't! Often it leads to injury, stress, and two very dysfunctional dogs.

Remember, your current dog probably believes he is in charge of your safety and the protection of your home, so he may not take kindly to the intrusion of a newcomer.

Regardless of how nice your existing dog is, it is best to introduce it to your Dane on neutral territory. Do this outside of your house or yard and have both dogs on a leash.

If possible, employ the help of a second person as it's important initially to keep them apart as you walk. Do this until they are comfortable enough with each other to make the usual "sniff" introductions. Keep the intros short and positive until they're comfortable in one another's company.

If you have outside space, then your yard is a good meeting place. Keep both dogs on a leash and allow your existing dog to be first on the scene. Bring your Dane into the yard to meet him.

If all goes well, let them sniff it out. However, at any sign of aggression or tension, separate the pair immediately. Allow things to calm down and repeat the introduction process.

Once the dogs are comfortable with each other, do the same thing inside the house.

Take Your Time

Regardless of where you introduce your new dog or puppy to your existing dog, it's vital to take your time. Remember, the pair are not only going to share the same space but also your affections.

Be aware. It's entirely possible to make your existing dog jealous by being overly protective of your new Dane. Dish out the praise equally, and eventually, they will sort out a hierarchy between themselves. Don't forget, though. You are the pack leader!

During the early days, when you are leaving your dogs alone for any time, keep them separated, either in their crates or in different rooms. This will not only prevent any fighting but also stop the newbie from picking up any bad habits from the older dog, such as soiling or chewing.

As harsh as it may sound, it's also to stop unsupervised shenanigans in the house too. When a 100-plus-pound Dane plus another dog get their "chase me" hats on in the living room, watch out!

On a personal note, our new Great Dane pup (Jax Teller) and our existing Field Spaniel (Cocoa Pop) didn't hit it off right away, and Cocoa took every opportunity to keep Jax well and truly in his place. This behavior was non-aggressive but continued even after Jax grew to be four times her size. We were lucky as eventually they became inseparable.

Unfortunately, this is not always the case and in extreme circumstances you may have to think about re-homing your new pet. Before you take this drastic action, though, seek the advice of a professional.

Cats

Great Dane puppies in particular are curious, friendly, and may assume all other pets want to play. Your cat, however, could have different thoughts on the subject, and "hey, let's play" is not always one of them.

Even as a lolloping bundle of baggy fur, your Dane pup will be heavier than most felines, and therefore intimidating. While it is unlikely that the puppy will intentionally injure the cat, a frightened or stressed feline can strike out and scratch your dog's nose or eyes.

Once again, a slow introduction is the way to go, and the first thing to do is to introduce the dog's scent into the cat's environment. Try wiping your dog's coat with a small towel and leaving it close to the cat's sleeping area. You can also leave something belonging to the cat near your dog's bed.

Face-to-face meetings should be with your Dane on a leash and for short periods of time. Keep reassuring your cat and make sure it has an escape route in case it's feeling unsure.

Keep some treats with you to reinforce good behavior in both animals and distract the dog if it's taking too much notice of the cat. Contain them in separate rooms for a few days, until they've become used to one another's presence, and don't rush things.

It's a common belief that cats and dogs are natural enemies, but they're not. They may never greet each other every morning like long-lost buddies, but they can live quite harmoniously under the same roof. Successful cat and dog cohabitation is based mainly on a healthy dose of indifference from both parties.

Livestock

If you live in a rural area where there are livestock, ask your neighbors if you can introduce your Great Dane to them. Let them get to know you and your dog.

For instance, if you live near someone with a horse, find out what time they go out riding and make sure you schedule your walks so you meet up. Keep your dog on a leash and at a distance from the horse. Reassure him while at the same time getting him used to this new type of animal. Dogs who are accustomed to seeing other large animals are less likely to lunge and bark.

Choosing A Veterinarian

Once your puppy or dog arrives home, don't waste any time in beginning the search for a suitable vet.

Every dog needs to visit a veterinarian, whether it's for vaccinations, neutering, or emergency treatment.

Even though all veterinarians are trained to set standards, some may be more used to treating regular-size family pets and may not be confident handling a dog the size of a small horse.

With this in mind, here are some tips on tracking down the right professional for your gentle giant.

- First port of call is to check out websites. Here, you can get a handle on the vet's personality and style. Plus, you may find information on prices and any specializations

- Don't leave finding a veterinarian until you need one. Immediately after you bring your puppy or adult dog home, register with a vet that is close to your address. Should you ever be faced with an emergency, you need a vet that's as close as possible and one that knows your Dane's history

- When you have found a place you like the look of, call and chat with the office manager to find out more about their services. It's also a quick way to experience their commitment to customer service

- Ask for recommendations from local breeders of all giant-breed dogs; they are likely to have a vet in the area on speed dial

- When you find a veterinarian that fits the bill, if at all possible, take your Dane for a visit. That way, your Great Dane won't form any negative associations and you can hopefully schedule a brief chat with a practice vet

- Try and build up a rapport with your vet. Remember, Danes are intuitive and pick up on vibes very easily. If you are not relaxed, then neither will they be

- Don't be afraid to ask questions. Your Great Dane is an important member of your family and it's necessary to understand the diagnosis and the course of treatment the vet is intending to take

- Ask about cost. It's not always possible for a vet to give an exact cost for treatment but they should be able to give you a ballpark figure for common procedures

Photo Courtesy of Nick Hudgins

- If you don't have pet insurance in place, find out if the practice offers any payment plans

Finding the right veterinarian for your Great Dane is crucial.

Start As You Mean To Go On

"If owner permits the young Dane to enter the kitchen, be prepared for 'counter surfing'. They can reach everything. If your Dane is allowed on the furniture as a puppy, then do not fool yourself that you will be able to get it off the furniture in the future."

Cynthia Neet
Neet Danes

Start as you mean to go on. Set the ground rules and keep to a routine.

Make it as easy as possible for your Dane puppy or adult dog to know what is expected from him, and what they can expect from you.

CHAPTER 5
Successful Puppy Parenting

Is Crate Training for You?

"If owner permits the young Dane to enter the kitchen, be prepared for 'counter surfing'. They can reach everything. If your Dane is allowed on the furniture as a puppy, then do not fool yourself that you will be able to get it off the furniture in the future."

Cynthia Neet
Neet Danes

Photo Courtesy of Deborah Hickman

The potential for controversy on this subject is high, purely because of how many polarizing opinions exist across the world.

In the US, crating is standard practice, while in the UK, it's just beginning to gain in popularity. For Scandinavian countries, such as Sweden and Finland, crating is illegal.

Living in the UK at a time when crating was very frowned upon, it wasn't an option open to us.

HELPFUL TIP
Training You and Your Dog

Oftentimes, socialization problems stem from untrained dog owners. Do not tolerate or induce aggression, dominance, or jumping from your Dane. Putting in the effort and time to socialize your dog will reap benefits in the long run. Be patient and consistent, and you will have a mild-mannered, agreeable companion for life.

Over the years and in the course of welcoming three Great Danes into our family, we've provided them with a number of different sleeping arrangements. These ranged from queen-size beds to under-stairs cubbyholes.

However, since moving to Greece, I am now a true crate convert. Over the last five years, we have fostered dozens of homeless puppies, and each time used a crate as a training aid.

Our other two adopted dogs, Gumbo and Bean, both sleep in one today. It's not unusual for them to wander into their crates and have an afternoon nap—with the door open.

The first thing to realize is that, when done correctly, crating is not cruel. Puppies are genetically predisposed to sleeping in dens from birth, so to a puppy, a crate is a safe place.

Here are just some of the pros to crating:

- A crate is a helpful aid in housetraining
- Until you can trust your puppy, crate training limits damage to your property and belongings when you are away from the home
- It can help to get your puppy into a routine, which is the single most important thing to establish

A crate should never be used as a punishment or have negative connotations for your Great Dane pup. It's not the magical answer to correcting bad behavior, and if misused as punishment, it can make a dog feel depressed, frustrated, and trapped.

Photo Courtesy of
Danielle Clarke

You should never leave your puppy in a crate for too long. Puppies less than six months old should spend no more than 3-4 hours crated at a time. They can't control their bladders for a long time. The same more or less goes for adult Great Danes too.

There are various options of crates available on the market today but for a giant breed dog, only one is suitable and that is a heavy-duty crate. This crate is ideal for giant breed dogs. It is also the best option for a dog that chews or is an escape artist. While in appearance, it's a little prison-like, it is the best option for your growing dog.

There are various options for this style of crate. Some have one door, some two, and many are collapsible. It is also possible to buy heavy-duty crates with dividing panels and covers. So do your homework and check out what is available at your local pet store and online.

Plastic crates, wire crates, and soft-sided crates are not the best option for a growing Great Dane puppy as they will not see them through into adulthood. Eventually, you will need a huge crate, so it's best to bite the bullet and buy the correct size from the outset. The crate should allow sufficient space for the puppy to stand and turn and be comfortable. You can reduce the size of the adult-size crate by blocking off any unused space and increasing it as the dog grows.

Danes are sociable and thrive on human interaction, so make sure to place your crate where your puppy can see you.

Crating gets a bad reputation from people who lock their dogs in them for excessive lengths of time. A crate is not a lockdown facility. It's a tool to help you manage your household and give your puppy a secure place where he can feel safe.

Never forget that in a relatively short time, a Dane puppy will multiply its weight and height many times over. Therefore, the boundaries and rules you set from an early age will be crucial for adequately controlling your 100-plus-pound adult dog.

Crating your Dane pup, if done correctly, will help equip him with a set of rules that will last a lifetime and make both your lives enjoyable. If done correctly, you will find your puppy voluntarily goes to his doggy den for a rest.

I wish crating had been an option for our current Dane, Jax Teller. Many times over the years, he has tried to crush his big behind into our Pit Bull's crate!

TOP TIP

Following the advice of a well-known dog trainer, we have used a crate to help get our existing pet used to new pups. Gumbo, our rescue Pit Bull, was extremely aggressive at first to puppies. She suggested we put Gumbo in his crate and let the new pup walk around the room for 10 minutes at a time over a week or so.

As time went on, the puppy got braver and edged closer to the crate. Over the next few days, Gumbo got so used to seeing the pup that he no longer growled or barked. His aggression turned to curiosity, and it wasn't long before he was either ignoring the puppy or playing happily with it.

Crate Training Made Easy

Whether you're starting out with a pup or giving an older Great Dane a new home, crate training will help you speed along the training process.

To recap, here are some basics for making crate training easy.

- Make sure the crate is large enough to accommodate your growing dog

- Buy the largest crate you can find and block off a section of the right size for your dog, increasing the area as he grows

- Make bedding inside the crate as cozy as possible

- From a practical point of view, try finding a crate with a double door, purely because it gives more options when placing it in your home

- Don't force your dog into the crate. Instead, use treats and encourage your Dane to check out the inside for himself and in his own time. Slowly build up his comfort level

- In the beginning, place a few of your puppy's favorite toys in the crate; leave the door open so he can wander freely in and out

> Hide a healthy treat inside, and you will find your puppy will soon come to regard the crate as a positive place!

> Leave the door open and only close it for short periods at a time, building up gradually. The aim here is for your dog to realize that it's not a big deal to be inside the crate because, at some point, you'll let him back out

> Place the crate in a high-traffic area so your dog can see all the family. The crate should never be out of the way so your dog feels secluded or isolated

> Avoid placing the crate anywhere your dog can see the outdoors. Danes can be vocal and may bark at any movement. You need to establish that when the dog is in the house, the outside world is not his concern

Dealing with Bad Behavior

Throughout this book, I will keep stressing the importance of repetition, control, and correct training. This consideration is important for every dog, but due to the sheer size of an adult Great Dane, being able to control your dog and correct negative behavior is particularly non-negotiable.

Repetition and clear instructions for your pup are key as you're laying the groundwork for a lifelong relationship that will not only give you immense satisfaction, but that is essential for the well-being of a breed that lives to please you.

But what if you've been a bit slack or your Dane pup has picked up a few bad habits before arriving in your home?

The majority of bad behavior in your Dane pup will come from anxiety, boredom, or not understanding what you expect of him. It may be that he doesn't initially accept you as his pack leader. Thankfully though, Great Danes are bright and, with a little persistence, can easily be set on the right track.

Let's take a look at the most common forms of bad behavior:

- **Food Aggression**
- **Chewing/Being Destructive**
- **Urinating in the House**
- **Excessive Barking and Whining**

*Photo Courtesy of
Colleen Pritchett*

Food Aggression

If your pup is snappy or aggressive around his food, you need to firmly establish that while you are the giver, you can also be the taker. At mealtimes, make your dog sit and wait. Ensure you let your Great Dane know that receiving food comes as a result of his being patient.

Stay close by your dog when he eats and occasionally pick the bowl up before he finishes. Make him sit, and then put the bowl back down so he can continue eating. This time is also perfect for reestablishing basic commands, including "Sit" and "Stay."

Chewing/Being Destructive

If your Dane chews your shoes or anything else for that matter, remove the item from him. Do this slowly and gently, as you don't want to engage in a tug of war! Replace the item with a good-quality chew toy. Give your puppy a couple of good-quality dog biscuits along with lots of praise for chewing the right thing. You can buy some chew toys that you push treats inside, which dogs particularly enjoy.

Chewing can be a result of boredom or opportunism. I remember waking up very late one Sunday morning to a grinding-crunching noise. On further investigation, I discovered our gangly adolescent, Billy Ray, had chewed a basketball-sized hole in a partition drywall, all from the comfort of his dog bed.

In this particular case, I moved his bed and made sure he had his chew toy with him at bedtime and sprayed the repaired wall with bitter apple spray.

Urinating in the House

If you catch your puppy about to pee in the house, distract him immediately with a clap or shout. Use a simple command like "No," and get him outside right away. Praise your puppy when he goes outside and reinforce that good behavior with a treat.

If you don't get there in time, clean the area thoroughly to get rid of the scent; otherwise, you're inviting the puppy to reoffend. You will need to use a cleaning product that breaks the mess down rather than masking it with a scent or fragrance. Also, do not use ammonia-based cleaners as they smell similar to urine and will encourage the dog to make the same mistake again.

Don't ever rub your puppy's nose in his pee or poop, and if you discover a "mistake" but didn't see him actually do it, don't shout or scold your Great Dane—he won't remember and won't understand that he has done anything wrong.

Urinating in the house may not always be a case of bad behavior, and could be more physiological. However, some puppies and even adult dogs will pee in the house to get attention.

Excessive Barking/Whining

Dane pups can be very vocal and may want to get your attention for a whole host of reasons, from the doorbell ringing to merely wanting you to play.

It may seem cute now, but Danes can whine to Olympic standards, and the sonic boom-like barks they produce in adulthood can loosen your fillings.

Use the distract and reward method, and if it's a case of attention seeking, your dog probably needs more exercise to burn off that excess energy.

Whining could be a case of your puppy thinking he hasn't had a good ear rub for a while, but it may also be because there's something wrong. Over time, you will learn your Dane's large vocabulary.

There are 101 different things your Dane pup can be doing in or around the house that are contrary to your house rules, but just remember he is still learning, and the world's a big place.

DO – Be patient. Patience gets results.

DO – Distract. It can be a clicker, a clap, or a vocal "No."

DO – Be ready with the treats to reward correct behavior. Great Dane pups love treats almost as much as they love praise.

DO – Give consistent and straightforward commands.

DON'T – Shout and scream. Great Dane pups are sensitive, and a happy dog learns more quickly.

DON'T – Lock your dog up somewhere as a punishment.

DON'T – Leave your Dane puppy on his own for long periods. Boredom can result in all kinds of bad behavior.

DON'T – Leave corrective action or training for another day. Great Dane puppies grow up quickly, and bad habits in big dogs are bad news.

Coping with Separation Anxiety

"Since your puppy is used to be with its mom and other puppies, being alone may cause it to react negatively to its new environment until they get comfortable."

Arthur Rivera
Royalty Great Danes

Dogs are social animals and love human company. You can pretty much double that for Great Danes, which is why it's easy to find yourself with a Great Dane puppy suffering from separation anxiety.

This problem can manifest itself in many different ways, from trembling and pacing, to howling and even wetting in the house every time you leave. Worst of all is the stress your puppy will feel from not knowing when you'll be back. This fear can lead him to destroy things while you're out.

This type of behavior, together with any number of other issues, can be relieved or avoided with help from your Dane pup's two best friends: repetition and routine. We all need to get out of the house at some point. Time spent out of the home is one of the main reasons behind crating (as discussed in a previous chapter).

Used correctly, with time spent in crate built up slowly and reinforced as a positive action, your Great Dane pup will come to learn that going into his crate also means coming out when you return home.

Strictly speaking, your puppy needs the social interactivity and stimulus of his new family, so he shouldn't be left on his own for too long in the first instance.

Whether you decide upon crating or not, there are still some basic principles that will help overcome their anxiety.

- Restrict your puppy to one room rather than giving him the run of the house.
- Don't leave anything you value lying around on the floor.
- Leave your puppy plenty of good-quality chew toys.
- Take your Great Dane outside for a bathroom break before you leave and again as soon as you return.

- Leave and return quietly and without any fuss. The jury is out on whether to say goodbye to your puppy, as many believe it can signal that it's about to be left home alone. Some animal behaviorists say a gentle and quiet goodbye can help to calm your dog before you leave. My advice here is, do what works for you and your puppy, but make sure whatever route you choose to go down, be consistent. On your return home, wait for your puppy to calm down a little before you say hello too. Easier said than done, I know!

- Leave a radio on low volume to provide background noise. (I've always preferred something like a radio talk show to TV, as there are no flashing images or sudden noises.)

- Practice going out for short periods of time to show your puppy that you will always return home when you leave the house.

Photo Courtesy of
Kala Fitzgerald

Time for Bed

Growing at an incredible rate is pretty tiring, and Great Dane pups sure do love to snooze.

Like all youngsters, though, they need to get into a routine and recognize when it's time for bed.

There are a few things to keep in mind regarding Great Dane pups and sleeping. Here's the lowdown on what to expect and how to get your puppy used to the idea it's bedtime.

- First of all, make sure your puppy has enough play and mental stimulation throughout the day.

- Don't feed your puppy very late.

- Around two hours before bedtime, remove water bowls.

- Just before bedtime, take your puppy outside for a toilet break and be patient. Don't give up until he has relieved himself. In the early days, it's unlikely your puppy will be able to go through the night without at least one pit stop. While you may be able to snooze through the whining, don't let your puppy suffer; bite the bullet, take him outside, and stay with him.

- Create a specific sleeping place where your dog can feel happy and safe.

- Put him in his safe place. Be calm and gentle as you settle him down for the night. It's a good idea to signal that it's sleepy time by turning the lights off. Great Danes (like all dogs) have more rods in their eyes (light-sensitive elements of in the retina), so they can see better in low light levels. You may think it's pitch-black, but your Great Dane will still have some night vision. This ability means that he's less likely to freak out because he's in a dark room. If, however, he gets agitated when the lights go out, you can always use a small plug-in nightlight or open the curtains a little to let in some outside light.

Tips:

- When we crate train our puppies, at night, we throw a blanket across the top of the crate to cover the back and both sides. We leave the front clear so the pups can see out. During the day, we fold the blanket back. Doing this gives them a visible cue. So when we pull the blanket over the cage, they know it's sleeping time. The blanket is also useful for keeping out any drafts and excess light and can help make the puppy feel more secure.

- My wife and daughter always sing to our more anxious foster pups at bedtime. It soothes them, can distract them if they are starting to whine, and reinforces that it's sleeping time. Although I was skeptical at first, I have to say, all you have to do now is sing a lullaby to our senior Dane, Jax Teller, and his eyelids start to get heavy!

When it comes to sleep, Great Danes are pretty much like humans in that they are diurnal. This means they have sleep cycles, so they are active during the day and sleep when it gets dark.

What does this mean to you? Well, simply this; training your Dane pup to follow a bedtime routine is not like teaching it to play the piano. You're tapping into basic genetic traits, and with some reasonably straightforward commands, it should go smoothly.

One last word to the wise, Great Dane puppies crave attention. When you're asleep, your dog may see this as a waste of valuable snuggling time, which is why at first he may whine like crazy in the middle of the night.

Do yourself a big favor and don't give in! Or else you're going to end up with 100+ pounds of smug-looking Great Dane sleeping in your bedroom for the next several years.

Home Alone

We all live busy lives, and there will be times when your Dane puppy has to be left alone in the house. However, when your puppy is very young (less than 12 weeks old), you shouldn't leave him alone for more than an hour or two at a time.

Leaving your Great Dane puppy alone any longer will upset him, and he will become anxious and stressed. Your puppy will undoubtedly soil himself, and you will pave the way for anxiety and separation issues further down the line.

In cases like this, you either need a dog sitter, friend, or neighbor (basically someone you trust) to visit with your pup. Not only will it break up your puppy's day but will also keep the toilet training ongoing. You will need to make sure your friends or sitters stick to your rules regarding commands and rewards, though.

As your pup gets older, he may be able to hang on longer before he needs to relieve himself, but any home alone time still needs to be strictly monitored and limited. Some owners return home for lunch or are lucky enough, as we were in the case of our second Dane, Billy Ray, to be able to take their dogs to work with us.

Great Dane pups are immensely sociable creatures and want nothing more than to be right by your side. You will cause them psychological damage if you leave them on their own for too long.

When you make a Great Dane puppy a member of your family, whether you're a single parent or have a large family, you must take into account that your puppy will need hands-on attention for at least the first six to eight weeks.

*Photo Courtesy of
Cassandra Harris*

CHAPTER 6
Nutrition and Diet

"You may have seen all the 'large breed' or 'giant breed' puppy foods out now. That's because giant breeds do have unique needs. Not 'more' but actually they need LESS of many nutrients like protein and calcium. This is to keep them from growing too fast. They grow very fast anyway, and too much of the wrong nutrients will cause their bones to grow faster than the tendons and ligaments can keep up, and can cause terrible deformities."

Barb Bristol
Symmetry Danes Dietary Needs

How much food should I feed my adult Great Dane?

On average, your Great Dane will need the same number of calories (cals) a day that you do. With the average Dane reaching 28-30 inches at the shoulder, your dog needs to take on a lot of fuel to remain healthy.

In comparison to their huge size, the breed as a whole has quite a slow metabolic rate compared to their body mass. It's vital, therefore, to avoid overfeeding your dog as this can lead to unwanted weight gain.

As a rule of thumb, an adult Great Dane of average size that is moderately active will need to consume approximately 2,500 cals daily. Just like any dog, though, the exact number of calories will depend on a dog's specific lifestyle.

Dogs with a more active lifestyle will need to take on extra calories. For instance, if your dog exercises for more than 2 hours a day, he will need to take on 20 percent more calories, taking his daily intake up to 3,000 cals.

Senior dogs with a more sedentary lifestyle will need fewer than 2,500 cals to prevent weight gain.

You will need to provide the correct amount of food for your Great Dane, so it's essential to monitor his daily exercise and weight and make any necessary adjustments.

If you are at all concerned about your dog's weight, it's a good idea to have a chat with your chosen veterinarian.

Photo Courtesy of Sara Santorelli

Choosing What Foods to Feed

Most owners and breeders opt for dry food due to its convenience and in terms of providing all of a dog's nutritional requirements. You'll find all the nutritional information on the back or side of the packaging, but basically, you need food that is around 24% protein and approximately 13% fats.

That's only a fraction of the story, though, as it's also important how the protein and fats are made up. Always look at the list of ingredients; the first 3-5 items should be protein derived from a specific meat base. In other words, proteins derived from animals, not vegetables.

Just as important is the amount of calcium and phosphorous the food contains. The amount per serving of these two minerals is vital to your Dane's skeletal structure, which has to eventually support your dog's colossal adult weight.

Too little of each and the bones will not have sufficient load-bearing strength. Too much of either can also impact negatively on your Dane pup's skeletal development. As a rough guide, you should be looking for a calcium content of 1.5% and a phosphorous content of 1.0%.

How Much to Feed

Age in Months	Amount in Cups* Female	Amount in Cups* Male	Meals Per Day
2-3	2	4	3
3-4	3	5	2
4-5	4	6	2
5-6	5	7	2
6-7	6	8	2
8-12	8	10	2
12-24	8-10	10-14	2

*Use a standard 8-ounce measuring cup

During adolescence, 12-24 months, your Dane will eat more than at any other time of his life. As previously mentioned, this is a guide. The reason it can't be 100 percent accurate is simply that, just like people, each Great Dane is different. Feeding amounts should not be set in stone, but rather constantly monitored and adjusted accordingly.

Female Danes are generally smaller in stature and therefore require fewer cups per meal.

When to Feed

Puppies up to the age of 3-4 months should have their daily food amount split into three equal meals so as not to overload their digestive system. After that, you can split your dog's daily intake into two meals a day, which can continue throughout his adult life.

Puppy and Adult Formulas

Most dogs will transition from puppy to adult formula at around the age of 12 months. Experts disagree as to whether Danes should even have puppy formula at all, with some saying they should be given adult food from the age of 2 months onward.

This advice is because puppy food (even some giant breed–specific) is a lot higher in protein. While this is acceptable for other giant breeds, protein levels are crucial to your Dane's successful development.

Some brands on the market today sell puppy food specifically for Great Danes, but once again, if in doubt, seek expert advice.

Adult Great Danes

If you are welcoming an adolescent or adult Dane into your home, find out what food he's used to eating. If you can't source that exact brand or your dog fails to thrive or shows signs of poor health, consult the rescue center, the breeder, or your chosen veterinarian.

Transitioning to new food should always be gradual as Danes are particularly sensitive to changes in diet. Keep a close eye on your dog during

Photo Courtesy of
Danny Smith

these transitional periods, checking skin, coat, eyes, and breath. Last but not least, monitor his stools, and if you see any changes in consistency or color, pay a visit to your veterinarian.

The majority of owners opt for high-quality dry food with the dietary breakdown, as mentioned above. However, there are some alternative nutritional paths you can follow when it comes to feeding your Great Dane.

Raw Food (Not Suitable for Dogs Under 9 Months)

This food is basic and uncooked. It's an unprocessed diet made up of natural ingredients. You can get as involved as you like with this method, ranging from ready-made to homemade.

Good-quality ready-made raw food manufacturers generally keep the ingredients as pure as possible. As a rule, all the ingredients, including human quality raw meats (on the bone), vegetables, and fruits, are minced or ground several times before being packaged.

The all-important nutritional breakdown, as well as its contents, should be displayed so you can ensure your adult Dane is getting all its dietary needs.

Raw diet fans believe this method results in fewer health issues, sleeker coats, and an improved immune system.

DIY Raw

This diet is pretty much as it sounds and involves buying all the ingredients such as bone-in meat, muscle meat, and organs. You can then add your vegetables (which some owners liquidize) and finally add some raw eggs, cottage cheese, or yogurt with a little olive oil.

Your dog will require certain daily nutrients, so before going ahead with feeding your dog a DIY Raw diet, first seek the advice of your veterinarian.

Foods to Avoid

"As a puppy, they should NOT be fed any type of puppy food. The amount of protein and phosphorus can do damage to a giant breed dog. Feed them an adult formula."

Loren Bengston
Glacier Danes

Great Danes may look robust, but their stomachs and digestive systems are both remarkably sensitive. Foods that humans can easily digest can be highly toxic to dogs.

Feeding your Dane human food from the table or giving him a little of whatever snack you're enjoying as a treat can be a bad idea. Not only can some foods upset his stomach, but they also have the potential to make your dog very ill, and, in extreme cases, the reaction can be fatal.

Below is a list of basic foods **NOT** to feed your dog:

- Alcohol
- Tea/Coffee or any food or beverage containing caffeine
- Milk, ice cream, and some other dairy products*
- Foods with a high salt content
- Bacon and fatty meat
- Garlic and raw onions
- Avocado
- Grapes and raisins
- Cinnamon
- Chocolate
- Macadamia nuts and almonds
- Any sugar-free candy, gum, or food that contains xylitol
- Sugary food and baked goods

All your Dane needs to stay healthy and happy is the right amount of correctly balanced food and water, and the occasional good-quality recommended dog treat.

Photo Courtesy of Vesna English

Note: It is safe for dogs to occasionally eat the following foods in small quantities:

Bread, cashews, cheese*, coconut, corn on the cob, coconut, fully cooked fish (bones removed), ham, honey, smooth xylitol-free peanut butter, unsalted peanuts, popcorn (salt and butter-free, air-popped), salmon (fully cooked), shrimp (fully cooked, shelled, deveined, tails and heads removed), canned tuna (in water), turkey (no bones), quinoa, and plain, unsweetened yogurt*.

Managing Your Great Dane Puppy's Weight

"As puppies, it is important to keep their growth slow or they can have serious growth issues. We feed low calorie foods with proper phosphorous to calcium ratios. The Dane puppies immune system is very compromised during their fast growth time (age 2 months to 12 months). Their energy is focused on growth, so, we must protect their immune systems by not overloading them and keeping their diets very consistent."

Cynthia Neet
Neet Danes

A Dane pup will grow as much in its first year as an average child grows in its first 10-14 years. There is no set rule as to how fast a Dane puppy will develop. This factor is down to genetics and nutrition.

While you have no control over the former, the latter is very much up to you, the owner. For advice about feeding your Dane pup, the best person to seek advice from is the breeder. They will know the food that works best for their dogs and, importantly, how much and when to feed them.

This rapid growth rate needs to be supported with correct nutrition. Too much and you are potentially overloading your puppy's growing frame, which will put stress and strain on your dog's joints and ligaments.

Too little and you run the risk of starving your dog's rapidly growing body and depriving his brain of the protein, fats, minerals, and vitamins needed to ensure the puppy develops properly.

Staying Hydrated

"Keep hand towels around nearby to wipe spit and water off of yourself after your Dane visits the water bowl. For whatever reason, they come directly to owner after drinking water and share their experience with you."

Cynthia Neet
Neet Danes

As a rule of thumb, Great Danes need around one ounce of fluid per pound of body weight daily. So a 100-plus-pound dog needs just over 10 cups of clean water per day.

You should always make sure that your Great Dane has access to fresh water and can drink on demand to avoid him guzzling too much in one go. So you need to top up your dog's bowl several times a day.

Very active or lactating dogs will need more, and puppies generally drink more water than adults.

Hot weather can lead to dehydration. Signs for this include:

- Lethargy

- Dry tongue and gums

- Rope-like saliva

It is important that if your dog is dehydrated, you don't allow him free access to lots of water at once, as drinking too quickly can result in vomiting. So if you think your dog is mildly dehydrated, give him small amounts of water every 10 minutes for a few hours.

Puppies: 1 teaspoon at a time

Adults: 1-2 tablespoons at a time

If your Great Dane drinks a lot more than the recommended daily amount, it could be a signal of an underlying health issue, and you should consult your veterinarian.

Understanding Bloat

"Any Dane owner needs to be aware of the symptoms of bloat, since when it occurs it usually develops very quickly, and is an immediate life & death emergency."

Barb Bristol
Symmetry Danes

Bloat, or Gastric Dilatation-Volvulus (GDV), is a digestive disorder that affects all dogs. However, it is most commonly associated with deep-chested breeds, including Basset Hounds, Dobermans, Great Danes, Gordon Setters, Greater Swiss Mountain Dogs, Irish Setters, Old English Sheepdogs, Standard Poodles, and Weimaraners.

GDV occurs when your Dane's stomach fills with gas and then twists. This twisting action cuts off oxygen and blood to the stomach, but it is the increase in the size of the stomach that signals imminent catastrophe.

The bloated stomach compresses other organs and blood vessels, eventually cutting off blood flow to the heart.

Bloat can happen quickly. Without immediate surgical intervention, it can be both excruciating and fatal. Despite years of study, no real cause has been identified, but several factors can contribute.

Bloat can be hereditary and therefore inherited from a direct relative (if you're adopting a puppy, quiz your breeder about bloat in its bloodline).

The problem can potentially increase in senior dogs and can be brought on by eating and drinking too quickly and/or exercising immediately after feeding time. Some experienced Dane breeders also suggest that a poor diet can contribute to an increased risk of bloat.

If your Great Dane is experiencing bloat, its discomfort will be very noticeable, but certain symptoms will be more apparent than another, including:

- Pacing and restlessness
- Painful extended abdomen
- Drooling more than usual
- Irregular or rapid breathing
- Shock

If you suspect your Dane has bloat, seek veterinary assistance immediately.

Helping to Prevent Bloat

Because it's hard to accurately pinpoint its cause, totally preventing bloat is almost impossible. Having said this, there are measures you can take to lower the risk quite considerably.

These everyday habits can help your Great Dane to avoid this life-threatening condition.

Post-/Pre-Exercise

As far as exercise goes, Great Danes are described as dogs that like to range. This giant breed prefers to wander freely rather than run around like crazy. If your Dane has been out on a long walk, make sure he is calm and relaxed for about half an hour before feeding.

It is perhaps more important that you prevent him from doing anything strenuous for around an hour after he's eaten too.

Gobblers

Some Danes are overenthusiastic eaters, especially if they're part of an extended canine family who all believe the first to finish gets more. If your Dane loves to gobble his food, this can lead to a build-up of dangerous stomach gases.

A slow-feed bowl does what it says on the tin, preventing your Dane from using that enormous mouth to swallow the whole lot in one greedy gulp.

HELPFUL TIP
Know Your Role

Your role as a dog owner is to be leader of the pack. Your Great Dane will need conditioning to become well-adjusted and a good companion. Know the methods of conditioning and utilize them correctly to give your dog dependable, clear messages regarding your expectations.

Spread It Out

Split your dog's daily meal allowance into two or even three meals, if you're concerned.

Water on Tap

Give your Dane free access to water so he can drink whenever he needs to. This access prevents him from building up a thirst and guzzling copious amounts of water in one go.

Surgical Option

In the last ten or so years, a surgical procedure called Prophylactic Gastropexy has become more popular with both vets and Great Dane owners.

In layman's terms, this procedure stitches the stomach to the wall of the abdomen to help stop the stomach twisting. It isn't foolproof and is not a total cure for GDV, but—and it's a big BUT—while not preventing bloat, it stops the condition from becoming life-threatening.

This surgery is not generally performed as a stand-alone procedure but is one that the surgeon carries out in conjunction with another operation.

This procedure is something that we opted for with our current Great Dane, Jax Teller.

I mentioned in a previous chapter that Jax once decided dish towels and socks tasted very nice. Subsequently, he was rushed to the vet and had to undergo an emergency operation to remove the offending items. My bad, I should have made sure these potentially dangerous items were not left lying around in the first place.

Before the operation took place, my veterinarian gave me the option for Jax to undergo this additional procedure to help prevent bloat.

The good news, he said, was that it was rare for gastropexied dogs to experience future bloat.

For future peace of mind, we agreed for him to have the procedure.

CHAPTER 7
Grooming and Care

"If you want your Great Dane to be comfortable with baths, nail trims and ear cleanings; do these things regularly and always positively reward correct behavior. This is an activity that I would be overly excited and boisterous with my praise for good behavior. I would offer their favorite treats and lavish them with love and praise at every small act of cooperation."

Brandy Massey
Massey Great Danes

Photo Courtesy of
Felecia Veneziale

Caring for Your Dane's Coat

Great Danes are short-haired, have a single-layer coat, and no subcutaneous fat layer. So what does this mean? Well, apart from not doing so well in the cold, their coats are pretty easy to look after.

Danes are moderate shedders all year round, with more molting in the springtime and, of course, short hair means no nasty knots or fur balls.

The first and most important step to caring for your Dane's coat is to ensure he has a well-balanced diet, because this is one breed where correct nutrition is the key to a visibly healthy dog.

As for caring for your dog's coat, you've hit the doggy jackpot. I have yet to meet a Great Dane that doesn't love a good brushing! As we all know, Danes are attention seekers, and grooming is another opportunity to get up close and personal.

Tip: Caring for your dog's coat is something that older children could get involved in too.

HELPFUL TIP
House-Training

Don't use puppy pads when training your Great Dane. Once he gets used to relieving himself in the house, it will be difficult to train him to stop. Avoid puppy accidents by keeping your dog's world small in the early months. His crate, water, and food should be placed in a small area of the home. Establish a schedule for your puppy, consistently walking him half an hour after eating.

Brushing and Bathing

"Brush often with a soft brush, boy does it bring out the shine!"

Jackie Herman
Ace-Hi Danes

While there are 101 grooming brushes out there to choose from, there's no wrong type as long as the bristles are firm enough to do the job but soft enough to make grooming a pleasant experience.

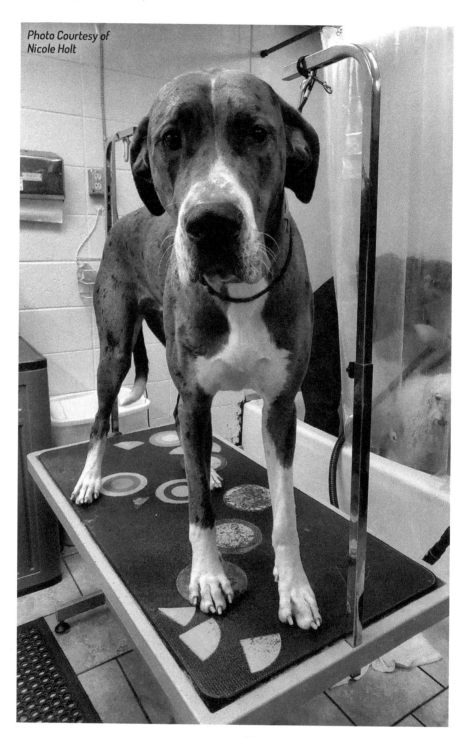

Photo Courtesy of
Nicole Holt

It's a good idea to gently wipe your dog's mouth and face with a clean damp washcloth before brushing to get rid of any drool.

Regular brushing and bathing will help to minimize shedding, so brush your Dane every day for a couple of minutes to keep his coat shiny. You can bathe your dog weekly up to every 6-8 weeks, or as needed.

Trying to get what may be an uncooperative fully grown Dane in the bath and keep him there long enough to do the deed is an interesting experience. Therefore you'll need to make bathing a regular occurrence and get him more used to the idea.

Here is some advice on how to do it fast and efficiently.

- No matter how stressful bathing is for you and your Dane, keep calm. It's important to reassure your dog that nothing terrible is happening
- Give your Dane a good brush before his bath
- Get everything you need ready at hand
- Use a washcloth or pet wipes to wipe gently around the eyes, nose, and mouth to remove any drool
- Keep water from getting inside his ears
- Make sure you use dog-specific shampoo and conditioner, NOT human brands
- Try using a 2-in-1 shampoo/conditioner. It can cut down on rinsing time
- Be realistic about the number of towels you'll need and then double that number
- Rub and air-dry your dog
- If you use a high-output hairdryer, be careful with the heat setting and keep the dryer moving at all times. You don't want to burn your dog
- After bathing and drying, use a grooming mitt and massage in a circular motion. Not only will this remove any loose hairs, but it will also stimulate the release of natural oils
- Finish by using a hydrating spray; this helps to lock moisture into the skin and coat

Tip: In the summer, my Dane prefers to be bathed in the garden with a hose.

Nail Trimming and Maintenance

"It is important to keep your Danes nails short. Long nails can cause pressure on joints in the foot and eventually lead to injury or cause arthritis. I recommend getting your puppy used to a wireless dremmel, it's the easiest way to do nails quickly and without the uncomfortable pinching of clippers."

Carrie Michaelson

Gem Danes

Like everything Great Dane, their nails are huge, but don't worry; help is at hand.

Generally speaking, exercising around your yard or garden or enjoying regular walks in the neighborhood will go a long way to keeping nail growth in check.

However, if like me you live in a rural location and your dog's contact with the natural filing action of a paved or concrete floor is limited, then it's important to inspect nails more frequently.

Let the nails grow too long, and you are promoting all kinds of potential problems such as bending back of the toes and uneven weight distribution on the paw. Unchecked, this problem can eventually lead to hip, shoulder, and joint problems as your dog has to redistribute his weight to compensate. So check nail growth every 2-3 weeks.

Follow these simple rules for fuss-free nail clipping

1. Make your Dane comfortable with you handling his paws and settle him into a position that he's happy to remain in so you can perform the task safely.

2. Choose what to use to trim his nails. A Dane's nails are super tough, so from personal experience, I would suggest the heavy-duty, scissor-style clippers in favor of the guillotine variety. You can also consider a pet-specific, Dremel-style grinder (providing your dog doesn't mind the noise and vibration).

Tip: To get your Dane used to the grinder, get some super-tasty snacks ready (Jax Teller likes xylitol-free peanut butter smeared on a dog biscuit). Turn the Dremel on and give your dog a treat. Feed the snack for 3-5 seconds. Turn the grinder off. When off, no snack. Turn on, snack, and so on, until your Dane looks happy when he hears the noise of the grinder.

Whatever tool you choose, you should only clip small amounts of the nail off at a time. Done correctly, the nail trimming process is painless. Done incorrectly, you can cut the quick.

The quick, just like in a human nail, contains blood vessels and nerve endings and grows in relation to the length of your Dane's nail. So cut too much nail in one go, and you risk cutting the quick. Your Dane will react by flinching, and the nail will bleed. Your dog will then also identify nail clipping with pain and discomfort. To avoid this, take your time clipping, especially if your dog has particularly dark nails.

Tip: I always have some styptic powder on hand to stem the blood just in case I ever do make a mistake.

If done carefully and regularly maintained, clipping your Great Dane's nails needn't be a big deal—for you or your dog.

*Photo Courtesy of
Breannah Milne*

Healthy Teeth

"Buy enzymatic toothpaste and get your puppy used to having their teeth brushed once a week."

Janie Pronto
Nuttree Great Danes

Many aspects of your Great Dane's overall wellbeing and fitness come back to one thing, and that is nutrition. A balanced healthy diet is not only the key to a healthy, happy dog but also equates to strong teeth and gums.

A Dane pup generally has around 28 baby teeth followed by 42 adult teeth. Keeping teeth healthy and in good condition is vital to your dog's wellbeing.

While cavities aren't a breed-specific problem for Great Danes, gum disease is an issue. Without the right kind of food, your Dane will have at best, bad breath, and at worst, a build-up of plaque leading to tooth loss and eventually gum disease.

Make teeth a part of your regular Dane check-up and look out for reddened or swollen gums, plaque build-up, and/or bad breath.

Brushing Your Dane's Teeth

Some owners introduce their Dane pups to the joys of tooth brushing. If you do this, you must use dog-specific toothpaste and a brush large enough to comfortably handle the job.

Brushing your dog's teeth is easy if you follow these simple steps:

- Introduce your dog to the flavor of the toothpaste by giving him a small sample to taste
- Gently lift his lip to reveal the outside surface of his teeth and gums
- Using a gentle motion clean the teeth and gums in the same way you would a child's teeth

Raw Bones and Dog Dental Treats

Saliva is nature's plaque preventer, which means a Great Dane should have the healthiest teeth on the block! However, when he needs a helping

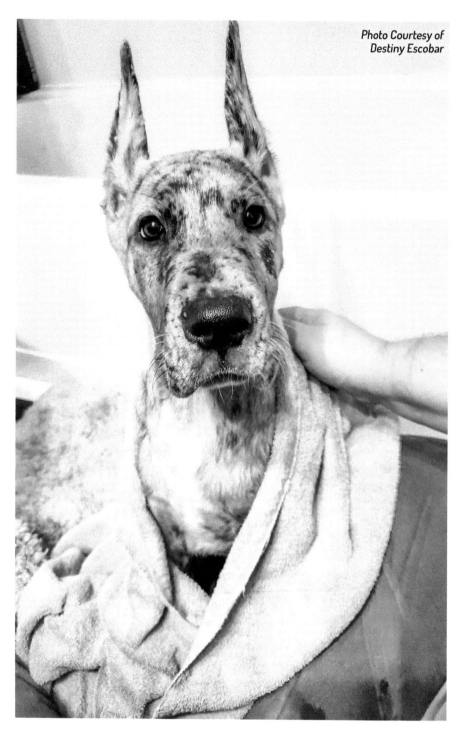

Photo Courtesy of
Destiny Escobar

hand, a good-size raw meaty bone or large dental chew is great for keeping teeth in good condition.

Apart from a balanced diet and the previously mentioned tooth brushing, raw bones, and dental chews, you can also buy specially treated wipes and oral sprays. These can help to fight plaque and prevent tartar build-up.

Drinking-Water Additives

If your Dane is particularly fussy about opening wide and saying "ahhh," you could consider buying dental additives to mix into his drinking water. Ask your veterinarian or trusted local pet store.

Professional Dental Cleaning for Dogs

Finally, you could book your dog a professional veterinarian cleaning. Your vet has experience in preventing and treating issues that you may not notice.

Bright Eyes and Clean Ears

While Great Danes are not overly plagued by specific eye problems, they are susceptible to certain eye conditions. Fortunately, these are easy to spot and, in most cases, treatable.

Carrying out a check on your Dane's eyes should be part of your daily ritual and can take a matter of moments. As your Dane lovingly looks up at you, use the opportunity to take a good look at his eyes.

At the puppy stage, Danes are just like every other breed, getting up to the usual mischief of sticking their faces into things they shouldn't. During this time, they're still at the learning stage, so get him used to you carefully wiping around the eye area with special pet eye wipes or a damp clean cloth.

This quick clean is particularly good for eye maintenance and will get rid of any mucus in the corner of the eyes. Tiny amounts of gunk are quite normal, but any build-up, over-watering, or changes in the color of the mucus can mean anything from an allergy to infection and should be investigated by your vet.

Warning Signs Of An Eye Infection Can Include:
- Tearing
- Cloudiness or Redness
- Squinting or Keeping the Eyelid Shut

- Crusty Discharge
- Loss of Vision and Focus
- Eye Scratching
- Distended Third Eyelid

As your Dane matures, he will become more susceptible to eye problems, so keep a lookout for drooping red eyelids and excessive tearing. This condition, ectropion, is often caused by the eyelid falling away from the eye.

Ectropion leaves the mucous membrane exposed, which leads to infection. The condition can be evident in one eye but more often than not occurs in both.

Ectropion is an inherited problem, which is yet another reason to quiz the breeder when you are looking to buy a puppy. While it is not always possible to see the puppy's father, the mother may be on hand to inspect.

This eye condition is usually a non-surgical problem treated by keeping the area clean or administering drops, but seek advice from your vet first.

Entropion is another condition concerning the eyelids but is generally more problematic as the eyelids roll inward, causing the eyelashes to irritate the cornea.

Dane pups developing this problem can sometimes grow out of this as their facial muscles and skulls quickly grow, but the condition often leads to eye correction surgery.

Great Danes can also be susceptible to glaucoma and cataracts. The former occurs when fluid isn't able to drain from the eye, causing pressure to build, consequently affecting vision.

The latter can appear as cloudiness to the eye and ultimately affects the vision as the opacity prevents light from entering. Either of these conditions can lead to blindness, so at the first signs of any eye problem, seek professional advice immediately.

Clean Ears

Great Danes' ears can attract a lot of controversy, mostly concerning the crop/don't crop debate. Regardless of whether your Dane's ears are cropped for cosmetic reasons or remain as nature intended, you will need to check your dog's ears regularly and clean them when necessary. This helps to prevent a build-up of grime and the likelihood of an ear infection.

The frequency of this procedure depends a lot on your dog's home environment. For instance, is it overly dusty or exceptionally muddy? Remember, as with all Great Dane–related maintenance, the more often they get used to the regime, the easier it will become.

Warning Signs of an Ear Infection Can Include:

- Head-Shaking

- Ear Scratching

- Rubbing Head on the Floor

- Swelling or Redness

- Ear Discharge or Foul Odor

As for cleaning, a good canine-specific cleaning solution is essential. The fluid is poured into the ear canal until it overflows into the ear. Don't squeeze too hard as you may introduce air pockets.

Massage your dog's ear at the base to make sure the solution works in and then stand back while he shakes his head like crazy. This head shaking will get rid of all the wax, dirt, mud, and gunk collected inside the ear, so try and do it outdoors.

Repeat the process for the other ear and then make sure both ears are wiped out and dried properly. There's an old saying that goes, "Never put anything smaller than your elbow in your ear," and the same goes for Great Danes, so don't even think about using a Q-tip, however careful you are.

If your Great Dane is excessively scratching his ear, there is discharge running from it, scabbing, redness, it smells strange, or your dog appears off-balance, then he may have an ear infection. Get it checked out by your vet right away.

Professional Grooming Advice

There may be occasions when grooming your dog at home is not an option, and for these times, you could consider taking him to a professional groomer.

Your Great Dane is an important member of your family, so the next step is to choose one used to handling giant breeds.

Grooming any dog is a highly skilled task and one that is not without its problems. Sharp scissors and electric clippers can be dangerous in the wrong hands.

So here are some basic tips to help you choose the perfect pet groomer

- While out and about, if you spot a well-groomed dog, ask its owner for a recommendation. If you participate in any dog training classes, ask the instructor and other pet owners for advice on reliable groomers in your area

- Once you think you have found a suitable salon, ask to see the facilities. Is it a place you would feel happy leaving your Great Dane? Are you able to stay with your dog while grooming is taking place?

- Check out the groomer's qualifications: Does the salon hold any certificates or accreditations? Are they a member of any professional grooming associations? Some states in the US require groomers not only to be licensed but also to have flea and tick application certification. So ask about this too. Most importantly, what experience, if any, do they have with Great Danes?

- Find out about their complete list of products and services. For instance, what products do they use? Are their shampoos and conditioners organic and/or chemical-free? How do they dry their clients? Can they trim nails, clean teeth, ears, and eyes, etc.?

- How do they secure dogs during bathing, and what sort of bathing facilities do they have? Are their baths large enough to safely accommodate a 100-plus-pound dog? Are the worktables and tubs sturdy? These are all things to consider when grooming a giant dog. You don't want your puppy to get used to a groomer and then have to move when it grows to an adult.

- When your dog is not being groomed, where will it be housed, and in the case of an accident, does any member of staff have first aid experience? Is there liability insurance in place should your dog become injured during any of the treatments?

These questions may seem very obvious, but it's easy to forget that while your local pet groomer may be confident in dealing with small and mid-size dogs, a giant breed is a whole different game.

The first time I took Jax Teller to a professional groomer, I chose one purely on location—big mistake. Jax was at the salon for just 20 minutes when I got a call saying he had dragged the groomer into the bath along with him and had pulled part of the ceiling down where they had tethered his lead to a flimsy overhead runner.

When I rushed over to pick him up, he was stretched out on the waiting area's leather sofa looking smugly out the window. The groomer was too nervous to move him. We weren't invited back!

CHAPTER 8
An Introduction to Training

Potty Training Options

Great Dane pups, by nature, are clean dogs, and the last thing they want to do is sit around in their own poop. Also, giant-breed dogs have larger bladders and will need less frequent trips outside, so house-training is often easier than it is with other breeds.

It is usual for it to take 4-6 months for a puppy to become fully potty trained, so the best time to start training is when your pup is 12-16 weeks old.

The first thing to do is to choose somewhere where you want your pup to go. This space could be in your yard or garden, in a designated room, or while on a leash.

Photo Courtesy of Melissa Mine

It's easier to keep one area clean than mine-sweeping every day, and also, the puppy will get used to having a spot. Once your pup has mastered that he must go to a specific place to relieve himself, then you can gradually give him freedom to roam around the house.

Whatever you do, if you find an accident in the house, don't rub your puppy's nose in it! Dogs just don't understand or remember why they've suddenly got a nose full of poop or pee, and it will confuse and upset them.

Wash the affected area well with a chlorine/bleach-free product that will get rid of the odor as well as the stain, so the puppy doesn't re-offend in the same place.

With puppies, it doesn't usually take long before nature takes its course, so be ready with lots of verbal praise and a small treat. Remember, between 8 and 12 weeks, your puppy won't make it right through the night without relieving himself, so be prepared for the night shift.

Apart from taking your pup out after mealtimes, show him to his toilet spot in between meals. Stay with him until he has relieved himself, however long this may take.

This is where crate training comes into its own as it can make the whole process much easier. At mealtimes, put the food in the crate with the puppy. When he has finished eating, remove the bowl, give him a moment to settle, and then take him to his potty spot.

Repetition and praise are the keys to this process, so be patient and consistent with your command words. Accidents are bound to happen, that's a given. Just say a stern "No" and return him to his area.

When you take your puppy outside, stay with him; don't leave him to his own devices!

For anyone considering using pee pads, here is some advice. Potty pads encourage your puppy to relieve itself in the house, which is the direct opposite of what you are trying to achieve. Also, your puppy will not understand why it is okay to soil inside the home.

Once you go down the pad route, remember, the time will come when your puppy is too large to be able to use them. At this point, you will have to fade the pads out, which is a hard undertaking.

Follow these simple rules, and in no time at all, you will have a perfectly housetrained pup.

Photo Courtesy of Sonia West

Housetraining Help for Adult Dogs

"Use a crate when you are unable to watch your pup. A crate is a tool for keeping your pup safe when you can't watch them; it should NEVER be where they stay for more than a couple hours at a time. Danes should never be crated for more than five hours a day."

Carolyn McNamara
Divine Acres Great Danes

You may have chosen to adopt your Great Dane as an adolescent, or given a home to a rescue Dane. Either way, you may be faced with a giant breed of dog that has incomplete or no housetraining at all.

Before we get into the subject of housetraining, we need to put on our pet detective hat, because there may well be clues that tell us why our adolescent or adult newcomer is urinating or defecating inside the home.

If your dog has wet more than once in a particular spot, it could be due to him smelling the scent from a previous pet and marking his territory.

Alternatively, depending where and in what conditions a dog has been kept previously, he can even develop a preference for specific surfaces to soil.

For instance, going inside the house can also be brought on by anxiety related to a change in the dog's environment and routine (or lack thereof).

In some cases, a dog may wet itself when playing, during greetings, or when he is told off. Consider also that maybe your dog has been taught to relieve itself on newspaper or a pad, and you, as its new owner, have suddenly changed the goal posts.

In all of these cases, it's best to go back to basics and begin housetraining from scratch. For this, you will need even more patience as with an older dog, you may be overcoming learned behavior.

HELPFUL TIP
Not a Running Partner

If you are looking for a companion to run with, a Great Dane is not a good choice. Danes do not have the endurance and stamina for long runs but do require a 90-minute walk daily, for puppies, and about a 30-60 minute walk per day for adult dogs. A large yard is a plus for Great Danes and their owners.

Consistency, patience, and reward will always win the day, so stick with the regime. To help with the process, for the first couple of weeks, make sure you can see your dog at all times when in the house rather than letting him wander at will.

Keep mealtimes to set times and take your dog out directly after feeding and at regular intervals throughout the day. Make new command words simple and easy, and be ready to praise and treat.

Obviously, you'll want to clean up the mess on a regular basis, but for the first couple of weeks, leave a small bit of waste behind in the designated toilet area. In doing this, you will encourage your dog to naturally return to the same spot.

If you catch your dog mid-misdemeanor in the house, don't scream and shout. Great Danes are sensitive creatures and hate being shouted at and

Photo Courtesy of Zadia Alden

may panic and run to defecate in another room. Distract your dog by clapping loudly enough to get his attention (or if he's skittish try using a clicker). Finally, without dragging, get him outside right away.

Giving a home to an older Dane is a wonderful thing to do. Just remember that he's got an awful lot to get used to, so be patient and repetitious until he gets the house rules down.

Be aware, though, that if your new Great Dane relieves himself in the house at unusual times or in odd places, the problem could be illness related, in which case you must rule out any medical issues by taking him to the vet at once.

Behavioral Training: Discipline and Reward

"Danes are fairly easy to train. They respond well to clicker training. Owners must be firm as well as loving. The Dane needs to trust its owner and that only happens by the owner being in charge at all times and setting clear boundaries."

Cynthia Neet
Neet Danes

The discipline and reward method is one of the most widely accepted and practiced forms of behavioral training.

The training and disciplining of your Great Dane is really important for several reasons. It will help your dog know his place within the new family (pack), and importantly, it will make things easier to manage when your dog eventually grows into the huge dog he is destined to be.

Amongst all the breeds, however, Great Danes are some of the most loving and loyal dogs. They live to please, and by giving them a set of guidelines to live by, you are contributing to their happiness.

Don't leave training too late, though; Great Danes can also be stubborn. So whatever method, commands, and rewards system you choose, do it sooner rather than later and above all, be patient.

Have you ever seen an unruly Great Dane? I have, and as you can imagine, 100-plus pounds of jumping, barking, and an out-of-control giant dog is not fun and also has the potential to be dangerous. Therefore, controlling the behavior of your Great Dane through training is essential.

Checking out all the different methods of training your Dane can be pretty confusing. However, what you need to consider is what you want from your Dane and the environment in which you both live.

As we all know, a Great Dane doesn't care where it is as long as it lives with you. Whether you live on a ranch or in an apartment is not the issue. However, it may impact on the level and method of training.

Fortunately, you have chosen a giant breed of dog that is both intelligent and lives to please, which is a good place to start. Bear in mind that whatever training method you choose to adopt, you are laying the foundations for the behavior of your adult dog.

The Reward Method

This method of training is tried and trusted. By communicating clearly and repeating the process over and over, your Dane will come to know what is expected of him.

As a reward for good behavior, your dog needs lots of praise, using clear, positive words followed by a healthy treat.

Remember, your dog is listening to you speak a foreign language, so make sure your commands are simple and clear. Stay patient and be prepared to go over and over the same thing many times.

Your Great Dane thinks in straight lines, and if obeying a command makes you happy and gets him a treat, it's a win-win in Dane world.

Punishment

Some dog owners believe that as the alpha, their word is law. There's no room for maneuver and failure to do as instructed results in punishment.

Yes, this method will eventually mean your Great Dane will be obedient, but it also reaffirms the negativity of that punishment. The dog is now responding to the potential of pain (either psychological or physical) for getting something wrong, rather than the pleasure and reward of getting it right.

For a breed that quite literally lives to make their owners happy, punishment is not playing to their strongest trait. Worse still, it may even lead Great Danes to associate punishment with all humans and not just their owner.

Let's get real for a moment: sometimes, our beloved Dane will do something so annoying or destructive that it pushes our buttons.

When this happens, train yourself to take a deep breath and count to ten before reacting. Regardless of which method you choose, screaming at, shouting at, or hitting any living creature is wrong, period.

Useful Hints and Tips

"The key to house training is prevention. Dogs naturally do not want to soil their homes. If your dog does have an accident, it is almost always because the human made a mistake!! Young puppies do not have much 'warning' before they have to go, so it is our job to anticipate their need."

Barb Bristol
Symmetry Danes

Photo Courtesy of
Chloe Shaw

Photo Courtesy of Danny Smith

So far, we've established just how important it is to introduce your new Great Dane to the rules of the house and establish a routine.

One of the best tips a Dane owner can pass onto to a potential parent is the need to establish a routine for yourself.

Everything to do with your Dane is XL, from the quantities of food it eats to the consumables needed to keep him in tip-top condition. It will make your life a lot easier if you have a regular checklist to run through.

That list should look something like this:

FOOD

An adult Great Dane packs away food like it's going out of fashion. Running out of supplies may mean resorting to buying something unsuitable in a local store to tide you over. Avoid this at all costs by buying a huge waterproof tub with a screw top. Every time you feed your dog, you will clearly be able to see how fast it's going down and will know how many days of food are left.

DRINK

Great Danes need access to water all day long, so when possible, keep your dog's water bowl next to the garden hose. Top the bowl up each time you walk past. That way, your dog will never run out of water.

THE END PRODUCT

What goes in sure enough does come out! And you seriously don't want to leave Dane-size mounds of poop hanging around. Buy a half-size garden trashcan with a lid and next to it, keep a roll of trash bags. The daily mine sweep goes in the bin, then when full, it gets tied off and is replaced by a new liner.

Important tip alert: Don't be tempted to buy an XL bin for this job; you will struggle to lift a full bin liner of Dane poop out of the trash can, and if the liner splits mid lift—well, don't even go there!

CONSUMABLES

If you use pet-specific wipes to clean eyes and ears, toothpaste, and shampoo/conditioner, keep them along with your grooming brush and nail clippers in one resealable container.

A tool tray with a tote handle is ideal. Everything is in one place, and it's easier to tell when you're running low on something.

One final word on consumables; get a dog-friendly antibacterial spray and keep it in your tool tray. Happy tail syndrome (HTS) may sound cute, but a room looking like a crime scene is no fun.

HTS occurs when the tip of a fast moving tail is damaged from impact with something hard. The tip gets cut, and as the tail continues to wag, blood is sprayed everywhere.

You probably won't be able to prevent it (can you imagine asking a Great Dane not to wag its tail?), but at least the antibacterial spray will help stop an infection.

CHAPTER 9
Raising Multiple Pets

Raising Siblings

Be very cautious of taking two Great Dane puppies from the same litter. Your breeder may try to convince you this is a good idea, but it can prove challenging.

Challenges of raising two puppies together include:

- Your puppies may fight over toys, food, and attention
- Two or more dogs have the potential to revert to a pack mentality

Photo Courtesy of
Katie Rischar

- Multiple puppies of the same age may get age-related illnesses or health problems at the same time. They could even pass away quite close together
- Should one pet pass before the other, the pet left behind may pine and become depressed
- Costs will double. These will include boarding fees, grooming, trips to the vet, food, neutering and spaying, toys, bedding, and more
- Adopting two puppies from the same litter will necessitate the help of a dog behaviorist and support from your breeder

Pet owners must spend one-on-one quality time with each puppy. Additionally, you will have to invest time into training each puppy independently. Furthermore, puppies will need to spend some time apart from one another. Doing this will prevent them from bonding more strongly with their siblings rather than with their human family

If you do decide on two puppies from the same litter, then remember pets of the opposite sex often get along more easily than those of the same sex.

Remember, dogs aren't like people, and they don't have a strong emotional bond with their littermates. They have no issue being separated and will happily settle as the only pet in your home.

If you do want your puppy to have the company of another Great Dane further down the line, a far better solution is to raise one Dane puppy to 12 months old before welcoming home another.

On the other hand, after 12 months you may be thinking of introducing another pet or other breed of dog into your home. If this is the case, here are a few things you first need to consider:

- Be aware that not all breeds of dogs get on well with one another, so do your research and take the personality of your first pet into account
- New pets, dogs or otherwise, need to be introduced into your home and to existing pets in a controlled and careful manner
- Animal experts recommend waiting 1-2 years before inviting a second pet into the home
- An animal may need up to 12 months to feel secure in a new home

Understanding Pack Dynamics

Humans and dogs have co-existed over many thousands of years.

Unlike other animals, dogs don't live in packs solely for the purposes of hunting and survival. Getting to understand their dynamic is important if you are to be successful in the training and managing of more than one dog in your home.

Given that humans and dogs have evolved together for such a long time, dogs' social structures are more like those of humans than wolves or other animals. Therefore, positive reinforcement training wins over training centered on dominance and punishment every time.

Photo Courtesy of Kathy Jerding

Understanding Multiple-Dog Dynamics

"It's important to always keep in mind that such a large dog can hurt smaller dogs by accident. Also, if a smaller dog attacks a Dane, the Dane does not think 'oh, this little dog can't hurt me!'. Dogs react instinctively, and the Dane will most likely defend herself. Which may result in the injury or death of the other dog, and the Dane will always be blamed even though she didn't start the fight."

Barb Bristol
Symmetry Danes

When you introduce more than one dog into your life, you need to be aware of the canine pack hierarchy.

When you have only one dog, this is simple. Human family members are pack leaders, and the dog is the subordinate. This dynamic is different when there is more than one dog.

Having more than one dog creates two packs with the humans again being the pack leaders and all the dogs, subordinates.

The dog pack, however, will establish the hierarchy amongst themselves. Generally speaking, a pack will have an Alpha female and an Alpha male.

If you watch your dogs, you can work out who is who in the pack by looking out for the following:

Dominant Dog Signs:
- Pays little attention to the other dogs
- Becomes jealous when you pet your other dogs
- Pushes his way to be first in or out of doorways
- Mounts the other dog(s) in the pack
- Exhibits aggressive behavior while eating
- Exhibits food guarding
- Leads the way on walks
- Sits in higher places while looking down on the other dog(s)
- Pushes other dog(s) out of their sleeping areas while claiming the best spot for himself

Photo Courtesy of
Carlee Caldwell

Submissive Dog Signs:

- Walks behind the other dog(s)
- Allows the dominant dog to take his toys or sleeping place
- Pays lots of attention to other dogs
- Licks the other dog(s) muzzle
- Lies belly-up
- Fails to hold or avoids eye contact with humans or dogs
- Submissively pees when he gets excited

If you have more than two dogs, then it is important to do things in the pack running order of first Alpha, second Beta, and last Omega. For instance, give all dogs the same amount of time and special treats but in that specific order. Let them in and out of the house in their pack order. Doing this will not only reinforce the dog hierarchy but also keeps the pack happy that they are all in the correct place.

In the event of the Alpha becoming insecure in his place in the pack, he may try to overcompensate by becoming more aggressive to reaffirm his dominance. Therefore by allowing your dogs to create their hierarchy, you will have harmony and balance not only within their pack but also in the family dynamic.

Addressing Multiple-Dog Behavioral Issues

My family's three dogs, Jax Teller, our senior Great Dane (Alpha); Bean, a female hunting rescue dog (Beta); and Gumbo, our male Pit Bull rescue (Omega), get along well most of the time.

Jax came first and is a born leader. Bean came second and bonded super-fast with him, and Gumbo joined our family a few years later. Gumbo came to us as a rescue puppy and had severe Ricketts. He couldn't walk, and our first two dogs quickly created the hierarchy.

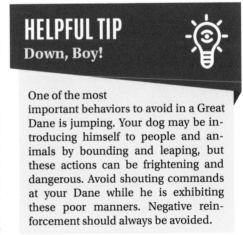

HELPFUL TIP
Down, Boy!

One of the most important behaviors to avoid in a Great Dane is jumping. Your dog may be introducing himself to people and animals by bounding and leaping, but these actions can be frightening and dangerous. Avoid shouting commands at your Dane while he is exhibiting these poor manners. Negative reinforcement should always be avoided.

Photo Courtesy of
Tamasin Pocock
Tamzdane Great Danes

We moved house recently, and this led the otherwise happy trio to feel stressed and act out. Stress can often lead to aggression and must be dealt with as quickly as possible.

FEEDING TIME

Problem:

Jax began to growl as he ate while casting sidelong glances toward Gumbo. This would cause him to spill lots of his food on the ground. Bean ate her food quietly with no problem from either dog, while Gumbo began attempting to wolf his down as quickly as possible. When Bean finished her meal, she would run to Jax's bowl and sweep up all the kibble he had dropped. Jax allowed her to do this, all the while glaring and snarling at Gumbo not to come near.

Solution:

These feeding issues were caused by a house move and change of feeding stations. To prevent this negative behavior, I set up different feeding areas for each of the three dogs in a triangular formation. Jax and Gumbo are now fed in opposite corners of the yard, and Bean is fed in a large plastic pet crate. I stand in the center while they eat, and if one of them attempts to wander outside of their area, I simply referee them back. Peace is now restored.

TIME TO GO OUTSIDE

Problem:

There is a lot more outside space to explore in the new house, and so the dogs are very keen to get outdoors. Each one began pushing the other to be let out the door first. Jax the Dane is elderly but has weight behind him, while Bean, as the smallest and most excitable, initially managed to run between his legs to get out first. This caused 75-pound Gumbo to go into a frenzy. Jax, as the Alpha, started to growl and snarl at Gumbo, trying to prevent him from going outside altogether at times.

Solution:

The house move resulted in the dogs having to get used to a whole new set-up. To avoid this frenzy, every time the dogs went outside, I reverted back to basics. Jax Teller and Bean immediately responded to being told to "wait" while Gumbo plowed on regardless. In the short term, I kept them waiting behind the dog/child gate while I let them out one at a time in pack order. They are now remembering they must calmly wait until released.

⊘PLAYTIME

Problem:

Bean and Gumbo love to play with one another. They bite and chew each other, and sometimes when they get overexcited and carried away, they border on the brink of nastiness. As Gumbo is three times Bean's weight, this once led to Bean's ear being torn and an expensive trip to the vet.

Solution:

Photo Courtesy of Jasinda Brown

When they get this way, Jax will stand over the pair snarling and growling until they stop. While it's okay to allow the Alpha to settle small issues between the pack, if the situation looks like it's escalating, it's time to step in and break up the party. You need to do this before it gets nasty. When this happens, I crate both Gumbo and Bean for several minutes to allow them to calm down before releasing them again to play nicely. Shouting at them can increase their energy levels and lead to a show of aggression, so I speak calmly and use my regular tone of voice.

⌒⌒⌒BEDTIME

Problem:

In the previous house, each dog had their own crate and would wander into it at bedtime. The crates would be closed while they slept. In the new house, the dogs sleep together in an area under the stairs, partitioned off with a child safety gate. There is a freestanding child's bed with a metal frame for Jax and two soft pads on the floor with blankets for Gumbo and Bean.

All went well in the new arrangement for a week or two. However, after this, Jax began to jump up on his bed, wait for Gumbo to get comfortable on the pad, and then decide he preferred the look of Gumbo's spot to his own. Jax would squeeze onto the pad, oftentimes sitting on top of Gumbo or trying to nudge him out of the way to create more space. The charade of bed to pad, pad to bed, carried on a few times. Eventually, Bean claimed the bed while leaving the boys to compete for space on the floor pads.

Solution:

I went back to crating Gumbo and Bean at bedtime for two weeks. After ten days, I left Bean's cage unlocked and then Gumbo's a week later. Peace is now restored and the bedtime competitiveness is at an end.

These behavioral issues were experienced just after our house move. However, they are typical of what you can expect from your pack of multiple dogs at some time or another during times of stress.

Although everyone's circumstances are different, the solutions I put into place for my pack are relevant to all dogs.

Dealing with Aggression

We now know that stress in an animal's life can lead to aggression.

Aggression between multiple dogs within the family unit is serious. If left unmanaged, it can lead to the injury or death of one or more of your pets, not to mention put you and your family at risk. It must, therefore, be dealt with immediately.

To deal with aggression:

- Strive to improve your pets' relationships with one another
- Manage and control your dogs' environment to lessen their opportunities to become hostile with each other
- Identify and eliminate your dog's stressors. These can be anything from noise outside the home to missing a member of the family or a combination of small issues which stack up. Learn how to identify the stress signs in your dog(s). These may include hackles up, lip licking, barking, growling, whining, ears flat against the head, visible eye whites, direct eye contact, etc.
- If the problem continues or escalates, seek help from an animal behaviorist

A few factors that could cause your management of aggressive behavior to fail include:

- Family members in the household who aren't following the plan/rules. It is vital that other adults in your home follow your lead. If they don't follow your plan of how to deal with the problem, they could undermine all your hard work and ultimately cause you to fail

- Toddlers and teens may not pay attention to your dog management plan
- Visitors to the home may neither understand nor comply with the rules
- Very strong dog(s) or those that are persistent in their aggressive behavior will seize the chance to breach your rules should the opportunity arise

Should you feel you can't rely on your ability to carry out the training or keep your family safe, seek the services of an animal behaviorist.

How to break up a dog fight

- Stay calm
- Do not shout or yell as it will only add to the frenzy

Photo Courtesy of
Brianna Montano

- Make no attempt to grab either dog by the collar as the dog (s) may whip around and bite you in the excitement of the moment
- Spray the dogs with a garden house or pour a bucket of cold water over their heads. Even a can of soda is okay if it's all you have on hand
- Throw a towel, blanket, or coat over each dog. Some dogs will stop fighting once they can't see one another clearly
- Put a barrier between you and the dogs. Anything that is available will work; e.g., a piece of wood or board or even a garbage can
- Once you have successfully separated the dogs, keep them out of one another's sight to prevent a further altercation

You may come to a point where you feel the situation is hopeless and start to think about either euthanizing or re-homing your dog.

Re-homing is not always a great idea as a dog with severe behavioral issues runs the risk of being mistreated at the hands of a new owner who may believe in physical punishment. Also, you could be passing the problem on to a new family and putting them at risk also.

Before you decide to go down the euthanasia route, remember that with careful management and training, the majority of dogs in these situations do greatly improve. In the majority of cases, they go on to live long and happy lives with both their two-legged and four-legged family members.

CHAPTER 10
Socializing with Dogs and Humans Outside the Family

"From 8 to 16 weeks of age, a growing puppy should see something new, and potentially challenging, each day of its new life."

Nathan Bolby
Grand Mimeux

Photo Courtesy of
Hayley and Jacob Duvall

Why Socialization Is Important

"As Danes grow so quickly it's important to start training and social-izing early. For the puppies safety you want to wait until fully vaccinat-ed before taking to public areas, but if you have family that have healthy dogs in a safe environment this can be a great time to plan a visit."

Carrie Michaelson
Gem Danes

Despite their enormous adult size, Great Danes are one of the most sociable breeds. If not socialized at the puppy stage though, they will struggle with meeting new humans and experiencing environments outside of the family unit. They can become fearful and aggressive. For this reason, socialization is very important. You must introduce your Great Dane to adults, children, and other dogs. If you do this, your Great Dane will be-come a confident and well-adjusted dog.

Dogs should be socialized from three to 12 weeks. A good breeder will have made sure that your puppy is used to being handled. Therefore, by the time you welcome your puppy at eight weeks old, he should already be tak-ing the first steps to socialization. This is one of the reasons why choosing a good breeder at the outset is so important.

Socializing your dog outside of the family is an ongoing commitment, and regardless of your Great Dane's age, you must carry it on throughout his whole life. Don't forget, every Great Dane owner is an ambassador for the breed. A well-behaved giant dog is not only a credit to you, but also goes a long way toward debunking the "big is dangerous" mantra of the ill-informed.

Regular socialization that is fun and not rushed means that your Great Dane will become a well-adjusted and confident adult. As with every aspect of his training, it's not something that will happen overnight, and you will need lots of patience. Get it right, and you will help your Dane to feel at ease in the majority of everyday situations and circumstances. Whether it's meet-ing new people, going to different places, or coping with new experiences, with correct socialization, he will take it all in his giant stride.

Socializing Your Dog around Other Animals

"Only introduce your new puppy to other pets you know are fully vaccinated and have a reliable friendly temperament. You do not want bad experiences to give your puppy a bad impression of meeting new animals. The more safe friendly animals the puppy can be introduced to the better pet he will be as an adult."

Brandy Massey
Massey Great Danes

Introducing your Great Dane pup to other animals outside the family is a must. Puppies have bucketfuls of energy, love to play, and between the ages of 8 and 16 weeks, they are at their most receptive.

Your puppy is ready to meet the outside world when he is fully vaccinated and has a correctly fitting collar with a suitable leash.

Take your Great Dane out to public places and walk him on a leash. If you go to a public dog park, don't go inside right away. Calmly walk him around the park first, and if possible, let him see what is happening inside with the other dogs.

Photo Courtesy of
Katherine Butt

Tips for introducing your Great Dane to other dogs while out and about

Take It Slow: It is important to have control, so both dogs must be on a leash. At first keep your distance from the other dog and its owner. Reassure your dog and reward him for being calm. Walk up to the other dog slowly. When they meet, allow them to circle and sniff one another. When this has been achieved slowly walk away.

HELPFUL TIP
Be Prepared

Great Dane owners are advised to have a "bloat kit" at home and while traveling. Owners should seek guidance from their veterinarian regarding the purchase and proper use of this kit. Great Danes can be prone to "stomach twisting" which is an emergency situation pet owners should be prepared for. It is always best to consult your veterinarian.

Confidence is key: During the meet and greet process use lots of positive reinforcement. Reward your dog to encourage him. This will make meeting new dogs a positive experience.

Don't enter into a tug of war: Pulling dogs apart or shortening the leash will cause your dog to behave negatively as this makes him feel frustrated and vulnerable.

Depending on your circumstances and geographic location, it may be possible to socialize your Dane with trips to the beach or the countryside.

A different environment will allow you to introduce your puppy to all sort of animals, from birds to horses, as well as sights, sounds, and smells. These new things all add to his socialization skills. Socializing with other animals outside of the family will help your dog to burn off all that excess energy too.

Allow him to walk on different surfaces too—sand, carpet, tiles, cobblestones, metal grids, wood flooring, and more.

Training classes can play an important part in your dog's socialization process. They are a win-win, giving you all the benefits of socialization as well as introducing the basic commands. For puppies, classes are great for teaching your dog his limits and how to be gentle when biting or chewing.

Meeting New People

"It's important to teach your dog to be comfortable around as many other people as possible. Keep treats in your pocket, and have strangers offer your pup a treat. Don't be disappointed if the pup doesn't want to take the treat, just give them some time and space. NEVER force a dog or puppy to approach someone they are afraid of. Interactions with people should be pleasant and not scary."

Barb Bristol
Symmetry Danes

For a Great Dane puppy, the world is new and strange.

While getting your Great Dane to mix with other puppies is important, making him feel comfortable around people outside the family is equally so. Take it slowly; it's a long process and one that should be continued throughout his life.

It's important to expose your Great Dane to people of all ages, shapes, and sizes. People wearing a hat or glasses, cyclists, rollerbladers, people in wheelchairs, or someone using a walking stick, etc. The more diversity, the better!

Photo Courtesy of Kristi Hasbargen

Monitor his reactions and if your dog barks, whines or stresses, stay calm, crouch down, and reassure him.

When you're ready, take your dog to small-size social events or out for coffee or to the store. Gradually build up to larger-size events where there are more people. Do this slowly and gradually, and you will build your Great Dane's confidence.

Take care not to overwhelm your dog, and try to make sure every new experience is a positive one.

Identifying Your Dane's Behavior

"Never forget that Danes are giant dogs, not just big dogs, and you will be held responsible for your dog's actions when out in the world. Make an effort not to put your dog in a situation where you are not 100% in control."

Janie Pronto
Nuttree Great Danes

While dogs may not be quite as complex in their behavioral patterns as humans, they do have their moments, and that is doubly so for Great Danes.

It's not always easy to understand what your dog is trying to tell you when he is outside the family environment.

Some signs of social anxiety to look out for are:

- Licking his lips
- Excessive yawning
- Whining
- Excessive panting or drooling
- Acting uncharacteristically
- Unintentionally relieving themselves
- Barking, growling, or lunging toward other people or animals
- Cowering behind you

It's not always easy to get to the bottom of the problem right away. If, however, you have continually socialized your dog throughout his life and outside of the family, identifying your Great Dane's behavior is significantly easier. The continued socialization of your Great Dane is not only of major benefit to him but is also strengthening his bond with you. Plus, it improves your understanding of him.

It is important to understand how your dog reacts to certain circumstances, and his comfort zone limits outside of the family unit. This skill will make it far easier to determine the reasons for his behavior and find a solution.

The process of elimination in identifying your Dane's behavior allows you to move on to the next important stage, addressing any potential problems.

All dogs are different, and even if you have diligently socialized your pup through into adulthood, they may still have triggers. These triggers can lead to certain behavior outside of the family home. Uncharacteristic behavior may even come to light as a result of some aspect or other of the socialization process.

Remember that if you have adopted an adult Great Dane, you may not have full knowledge of what his past experiences were. He may not have been well socialized in his previous home, so it is best to begin the socialization process from scratch.

Be mindful that he may have had a bad experience in the past with specific stressors outside the home. Be gentle and try to only introduce him to one external factor at a time.

Either way, socializing your Great Dane will give you the skills to identify the behavior and allow you to address it as required.

Photo Courtesy of
Melissa Miner

CHAPTER 11
Traveling with Your Great Dane

"If you are happy to make room in your home for a Great Dane I would strongly recommend planning to travel with them. Great Danes become so attached to their family they literally mourn when left behind."

Brandy Massey
Massey Great Danes

Photo Courtesy of
Katherine Butt

Preparing to Take to the Road with Your Great Dane

"Our dogs travel well in the car, use the bathroom at rest stops with ease, and generally seem to appreciate the change in scenery as much as we do."

Nathan Bolby
Grand Mimeux

At some point, you will need to transport your Great Dane. While trips to the vet or groomer may be comparatively short, you may at some time want to take him on a family road trip.

No two Danes are the same when it comes to traveling in vehicles. Some love it and will jump right in the moment you pop the door, while others need a three-man lifting team and the mother of all treats as an incentive.

For Great Danes, it's all down to negative associations, and if the only time you drive your dog is to the veterinarian, you can understand his reluctance.

Your dog being anxious in your vehicle can mean a lot of whining, barking, and fidgeting, which not only is obviously distressing to him but can also be very distracting to the driver.

On the subject of distractions, it's not advisable to have your Dane loose in your vehicle, unless you want those huge slobber-filled jowls resting lovingly on top of your head. Great Danes have little respect for personal space and no idea of their physical size.

So what can you do to fix this? First of all, if you're planning a road trip, you're going to have to build up your dog's tolerance. Begin by acclimatizing him to getting in and out of the vehicle.

Start out with a few short journeys and slowly build up the travel time. Take a few trips to places you know your dog likes, such as the park or beach, as this will give road travel a positive association.

If it's warm inside the vehicle, make sure you've got the AC blasting through to the rear. If you don't have air conditioning, open the car windows a little.

Photo Courtesy of
Chloe Morgan

WARNING: Never leave your dog unattended in a car. Ever. No exceptions, but especially not in hot or cold weather.

Things you can buy to make road travel easier for you and your Great Dane:

- A dog car ramp to help your Great Dane get in and out of higher vehicles

- A dog car barrier to fit your particular vehicle. These are generally available in mesh or metal

- A dog car harness

- Seat belt for dogs

- Space permitting, a plastic travel crate. Check on its weight restrictions as most accommodate dogs of up to 100 pounds

- A suitable car seat cover (s), to keep your seats hair and scratch free

- Dog treats to encourage your Great Dane to get in or out of the vehicle

- Pet wipes, pee pads, or newspapers in case of car sickness

- Poop bags in case of accidents

- A warm blanket

- Dog food and bottled water plus collapsible dog bowls

- Toys for longer journeys

When you pull over or arrive at your destination, make sure your Great Dane is wearing his collar, ID tag, and leash before you open the car door to let him exit. That way, if he manages to break free, he will be recognized as an owned dog rather than a stray

HELPFUL TIP

Great Danes are heavy shedders and should be brushed weekly with a firm bristle brush. Because of the size and weight of adult Great Danes, many owners opt to have bathing and nail trims done by a professional. A Great Dane's ears should be checked often and with great care to avoid infections and damage.

Pre-Road Travel Safety Tips

We have already covered how to keep your Great Dane safe in your vehicle during road travel.

Here are some useful pre-travel tips for when you and your Great Dane head out onto the highway for longer journeys.

- Microchip your dog. That way, if your Great Dane wanders off and gets lost, a microchip can help speed your finding him. A microchip is inserted under your dog's skin. Each chip has a unique number, which via a database has your pet and owner information. The chip is then scanned, and hey presto, the database reveals your contact details.

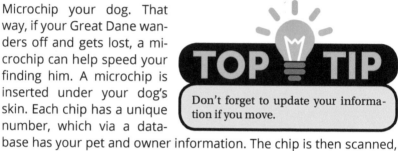

Don't forget to update your information if you move.

- Vaccinations should always be up to date regardless of travel plans. So depending on where you are heading for, chat with your vet and find out if your dog needs any additional vaccines. Some vaccines require a series of injections before they are effective, so don't leave this until the last minute. When everything is up to date, don't forget to pack your dog's vaccination paperwork along with any medical history

- Flea and tick treatments should also be current, especially if you are traveling to a hot climate. Check with your vet before you travel

- Anti-car sickness medication. If your Great Dane suffers from car sickness, leave a 30-minute gap between mealtime and a journey by road. Your vet can advise on motion sickness medication

- A first-aid kit for you and your dog is a sensible idea

- Pack your dog's regular food and treats. Take enough food with you for the total duration of your trip, along with a little extra. Your Great Dane will be experiencing a whole new world, so make sure his food is familiar. Firstly, you may not be able to buy the same type or brand when you arrive, and also, he may have an upset stomach from the journey

Plan your journey well ahead, and as they say, hope for the best while preparing for the worst!

Danes on Planes

Looking online for airlines that carry giant-breed dogs is a roller coaster ride. All too often, you'll see the claim "Yes, we fly pets" only to click on the "for more details" link and see the words "provided your dog/cat can fit in a carrier and under the seat in front of you."

Failing that, there's usually a maximum pet weight of 16 pounds, which considering an eight-week-old Great Dane puppy can exceed this without even trying, makes it a non-starter.

What you will need to do is search for airlines that carry pets in the hold.

Do's and Don'ts

Once you've found your carrier, look for the airline's list of Do's and Don'ts relating to secure crating. These will give you information on what you can and can't put in the crate with your dog.

For instance, you may want to put your dog's favorite toy in the crate with him to keep him company during the flight. Airlines class this as a choking hazard. Instead, consider adding a small blanket or one of your well-worn, unwashed T-shirts to the crate. Your dog will feel comforted by the familiarity of your scent.

You should also line the floor with plenty of absorbent pet pads, too, just in case.

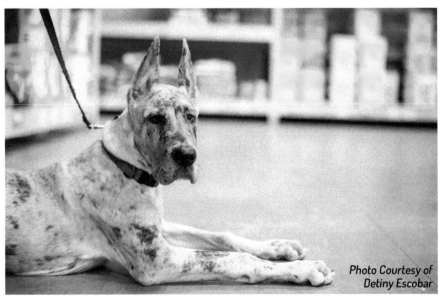

Photo Courtesy of Detiny Escobar

Photo Courtesy of
Enya Griffin

Pet Carriers

As with all dog crates and carriers, it will need to be large enough for your Great Dane to stand and turn around in, so strictly speaking, he'll have more room than you in coach!

Your dog's crate also needs to:

- Be durable

- Have strong handles, ideally on the top and side

- Have a leakproof, padded base

- Have ventilation on opposite sides

- Be clearly marked with a "Live Animal" sign and with arrows showing which way is upright. It also needs a label stating your name, address, destination, and full contact information

When you have bought a suitable crate, it's a good idea to let your dog get used to it by crating him in the travel carrier at home in the weeks leading up to your flight.

Food and Drink

As for feeding, you don't want your dog sitting in his own poop for hours. If he's been correctly crate trained, this ideally shouldn't happen, but even so, to avoid air-motion sickness, it is best to leave 4-6 hours between food and flying.

Dogs should be hydrated for the entire trip. Having a travel water bowl that dispenses a small amount of fluid at a time is ideal.

Sedating Your Great Dane

You may think that you're doing your Great Dane a favor by sedating him pre-flight. However, many airlines forbid sedating animals for flight. This is because sedating your dog can lead to them being sick during the flight, having a fatal reaction due to the drugs and changes in air pressure, or suffering a loss of balance during transport.

TOP TIP

If your dog must be sedated for any medical reason, make sure you have a letter from the vet explaining the reasons why. I once flew a foster dog from Greece to Germany. He was blind due to a brain tumor and was traveling for an emergency operation, so had to be sedated for the journey. If I hadn't had the necessary documentation from the veterinarian, he wouldn't have been able to fly.

Don't Forget the Paperwork

Depending on the destination, some airlines will require full documentation, including pet passports and microchips. Take the originals of every piece of paper relating to him, but have copies of everything in case they'll accept them instead. Check individual airlines for a list of the documentation you will require.

You will also need contact addresses and numbers for both ends of the journey. Make sure your dog has his contact details in a number of places on the crate too.

While this information covers the basics, you may have more specific questions about putting your Great Dane on a plane; these can be answered by the airline.

If you find the whole process overwhelming, there are companies that specialize in flying dogs and other animals. They will take care of everything, including the travel crate. All you need to do is go online and do a little research.

Hotel and Accommodation Stays

While a large number of hotels may proclaim themselves "pet friendly," it's often more of a case of "Yes, we'll take Fifi the Yorkshire Terrier" rather than Jax Teller, the adult Great Dane.

Having said this, though, a lot of "pet-friendly" hotels may not ask for exact details of your dog as long as you agree to pay any supplements or non-refundable deposits they require. These can differ in price from a $5 supplement to a $50+ NRD (non-returnable deposit).

When you're traveling cross-country with your Great Dane, the chances are you'll be staying at a roadside hotel or motel. For easy access, if possible, try and get a ground floor room, not because you need to sneak your four-legged friend in and out of your room, but simply because lots of Great Danes aren't crazy about walking upstairs. And an elevator may be a whole new experience for him!

When you find yourself in a dog-friendly hotel, walk your dog around the car park or grounds. It's a great opportunity to get

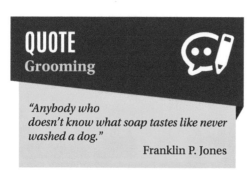

QUOTE
Grooming

"Anybody who doesn't know what soap tastes like never washed a dog."

Franklin P. Jones

him used to his new environment and to allow other guests to see how well behaved this giant breed really is.

Whenever you're out in public with your Great Dane, you are a brand ambassador, so show him off. It doesn't hurt to be seen carrying a large plastic bag (poop sack) around either.

As well behaved as your dog may be, don't be tempted to leave him in the room on his own. Unfamiliar surroundings and noises are, in all likelihood, going to result in him barking.

If you are confident enough or have no choice other than to leave him on his own, make sure he has a good chew toy. Also, leave the radio or TV on, and put the "Do not Disturb" sign on the door.

If your accommodation's policy doesn't allow pets to be left alone in your room, you are going to need to find pet-friendly restaurants. Ask the hotel for a list of suitable places that are nearby and do some research before you travel.

Always take dog towels with you during a walk so you can clean your dog's paws before entering the room. As well as avoiding muddy paw prints on the carpet, it will also be useful in catching or wiping off far-flung drool from the walls.

It's also a good idea to pack a couple of old sheets to place on the floor or bed. Also, make sure your dog's flea and tick regime is up to date. If it's a pet-friendly hotel, chances are previous pets may have left a few little friends behind in the soft furnishings.

While on the subject of furnishings, you could also pack a pet hair removing roller to get rid of any unwanted dog hairs.

Last but not least, make sure your Dane is well groomed and smells good. First impressions count, and if the hotel staff has a positive experience with their giant guest, it will make it easier for the next Great Dane owner to receive a warm welcome.

Kennels versus Dog Sitters

It's a big deal trusting the care of your Great Dane to someone else; after all, he's a member of the family. You share a strong bond, so it stands to reason you want the least stressful option for you both when you need to leave your home overnight or longer.

Your two main options are kenneling or a dog sitter.

Dog Boarding Kennels

Kennels can be quite traumatic for an adult Great Dane if he's never experienced one before. All of a sudden, he will find himself in an enclosed and confined space without his family and a lot of strange dogs barking like crazy 24/7.

The experience is much easier for a dog that has been boarded from a young age or one that is kenneled with another dog in his pack.

You may be fortunate enough to find a home boarder. This scenario is a case of your Great Dane being one of a small group of dogs which may include the owner's own pets. It provides more of a home-style environment.

If you are considering boarding:

> Ask for personal recommendations from any other Great Dane owners you may know, or ask your veterinarian or breeder

> Make sure the kennel is used to boarding giant breeds

> Ask to view the boarding kennel facilities, including the exercise areas and sleeping quarters. Find out about heated and air-conditioned facilities

> Some kennels, for an additional fee, offer added exercise options such as long forest or beach walks

> Ask if the boarding kennels offer grooming prior to collection

> Check out the kennel's itinerary for feeding times, exercise times, etc.

> Some kennels give you a daily price, which includes food. Ask for a price minus food and instead supply your own

> Make sure the kennel has its own vet, or if distance allows, your regular vet's off-hours number.

> Leave a contact number for your veterinarian

> Tell the kennel you want to know if there's even the slightest problem

> See if they'll send photos to your phone every other day or so

> Make sure you take your dog's favorite bedding and toys

Dog Sitters

This second option is preferable to a lot of people who've had negative experiences with boarding kennels or feel their Great Dane will be anxious in a regular kennel.

If this is the case, it makes sense to get someone to look after him in a home environment. The sitter may stay in your home, or your dog may go to theirs.

Although a popular choice, there's also a lot to consider with this option too.

> For this solution to be a success, your Great Dane will need to be well-trained and socialized

> When you go down this route, personal recommendations are best, so ask around

> If the sitter isn't a friend or family member ask for references—and follow up with them.

> Make sure your sitter is comfortable and experienced with giant-breed dogs

> Arrange for the sitter to meet your Great Dane before you book their services. Also, if your Great Dane is going to stay with them, visit their home to see their facilities and set-up. It is important to make sure they are a good fit with your dog

> Make detailed notes for your dog's food and daily routine while keeping your instructions short and factual

> Add additional info relating to his favorite toys, how he walks on the leash, if and when he is crated, when he's allowed treats, etc. Be honest—if your Great Dane pulls like an entire team of Huskies on the leash, don't say "he can be a bit lively!"

> Make sure your dog has an ID tag on his collar with up-to-date contact details

> Supply a list of emergency contact numbers including the veterinarian and a full itinerary of where you are staying at all times

> Don't book a dog sitter that you don't know at the last moment. Arrange it well in advance to give you time to build up a rapport

Regardless of whether you have a good boarding kennel you depend on or a dog sitter you can trust, the most difficult part for you will be letting go of the leash.

Don't make a big deal of saying goodbye to your Great Dane and try not to worry. Provided you have done everything to make sure he is in good hands, the experience for you both will be a positive one.

CHAPTER 12
Healthy Body, Healthy Mind

"Danes are a relatively low metabolism breed. 20-30 minutes of exercise generally is adequate. Walking with them is a great way to help them get exercise. We don't recommend running/jogging with them until they are over 18 months of age due to their rapid growth. They can run and play on their own but don't take them on long runs when they are young."

Loren Bengston
Glacier Danes

Photo Courtesy of
Enya Griffin

Photo Courtesy of Caroline Cannon

How Much Exercise Does an Average Great Dane Need?

Great Danes have a wonderful relaxed attitude toward exercise, and many like nothing more than to be dedicated couch potatoes. Don't get me wrong though, they aren't lazy dogs and the moment you reach for that leash, your dog will be ready to jump down from his favorite spot on the sofa.

Too much slouching around may cause your dog to pile on the pounds. Also, without building up your Great Dane's cardiovascular system and the muscles needed to carry his giant frame, you may be shortening his life span. Physical exercise gets the blood pumping and tones the muscles. Walking is also good for your dog's socializing skills and provides mental stimulation.

Your Great Dane's exercise regime doesn't need to be anything drastic and can consist of 30-60 minutes per day and should, whenever possible, be off-leash as this gives them the freedom to run free and burn off excess energy. Don't forget, before you exercise your Great Dane, you must leave a 60-minute gap before and after feeding.

Not all Great Danes have the same energy levels and their exercise needs will vary from dog to dog, so be sure to monitor this closely and adjust your routine accordingly.

Once your Great Dane reaches two years old, when most of his growing is done, you can introduce him to the world of sport and games too.

Photo Courtesy of Ashlynn Pool

Despite their size these gentle giants excel at all sorts of activities.

- **Weight Pulling:** This is the canine equivalent of a tractor pull. The jury is out on this one. Some critics say it can cause severe harm to an animal such as muscle tears, strains, and joint damage, while others believe it's a good workout and helps with aggression issues. One thing is for sure, before embarking on an activity such as this, make sure your dog is fit and healthy and chat with your local veterinarian.

- **Tracking:** Great Danes love to sniff and smell, and tracking is a great way for you and your dog to explore the outdoors together. You can get lots of fresh air and your dog can do what comes naturally!

- **Agility Sports:** Despite their huge size your Great Dane can crawl through a tunnel just as well as any other dog. Just remember, obstacles will need to be extra large to accommodate their weight and size!

- **Dock Diving:** This is a sport where dogs compete in jumping either for height or distance from a dock into deep water. So if you have a Great Dane that loves to run, jump, and swim he will have lots of fun with this activity!

All of these are activities that you and your Great Dane can enjoy together, which once again will help to strengthen the bond you both share.

Take your dog for a run on the beach, or let him blow off steam in a dog park, but keep a watchful eye for signs of over-tiredness. Tired Great Danes can quite literally trip over their own paws and tire very quickly if they are running around with smaller dogs.

Be careful not to over-exercise your Great Dane puppy either. Keep his exercise gentle and minimal until around 18 months of age. Due to rapid growth, you may overtax his hips, joints, and tendons if he exercises too vigorously when he's young. As a guide, puppies and adolescents need approximately 90 minutes of exercise daily.

Following a regular exercise routine will make sure your Great Dane has not only a healthy body but also a healthy mind all the way from puppy to adulthood.

HELPFUL TIP
Call Ahead

If you plan on traveling with your Great Dane, call ahead well in advance to find pet-friendly accommodations. Ask about weight and size restrictions at hotels. Great Danes may be difficult to travel with, so search out options such as a pet sitter or boarding facilities.

Suitable Exercises to Try Out

"Danes are generally considered to be a 'moderate activity' breed. There is a wide variation within the breed though, with some Danes being true 'couch potatoes' and others being very, very lively and active and energetic."

Barb Bristol
Symmetry Danes

A decent walk once a day is the minimum exercise your Great Dane needs to keep in shape, but if it's feasible, why not split his walk time and take him twice a day? It equates to the same amount of exercise but supplies twice the mental stimulation.

If your Great Dane is well behaved off-leash, why not take advantage of those crazy long legs and lengthy gait and cycle with him? You can cover longer distances; just keep the pace to a fast walk or trot. He should not be pounding his paws as this can put too much strain on joints and tendons, so make sure he is comfortable with the speed you're riding.

Photo Courtesy of Carly Angvick May

Regular dog leashes are not appropriate for cycling alongside your dog. There are a number of different types of leashes on the market today that are specifically designed for this purpose. You will need to thoroughly research either online or by chatting with your local pet store before you make your purchase. The type of leash will depend on your particular model of bicycle.

If you are lucky enough to live near a beach, you're in the perfect location to exercise your Great Dane. Sand provides a cushioning effect, which means the initial jolt of each paw-fall while running is lessened. This shock-absorbing action means less impact stress on hips, shoulders, ankles, and knees. As a bonus, sand also provides more resistance underfoot than other surfaces, so will give his muscles a workout, too. Whenever possible, avoid high-impact exercise on hard surfaces.

Having owned other smaller dogs at the same time as our Great Danes, seeing them run and play together is a wonderful thing. While the likes of our Cretan Hound can quite literally run circles around other dogs, just like children, Great Danes never know when enough is enough.

Letting your dog run with others together on grass either in the park or in your garden is fine as like sand, it makes for great shock absorption. Be aware though, when running with more agile dogs, your Great Dane will attempt to keep up.

This overexertion poses a potential problem, especially when your Great Dane tries to change direction quickly as this can be hazardous to long, gangly legs. Supervise play whenever possible and bring your Great Dane inside to rest before he shows signs of struggling.

Throwing games are great for your Great Dane, too, as it means they can fetch and return at their own pace. When playing this game, throw a heavy stick, as it will land and stay where it is. It means your dog won't have to change direction to chase the stick as it bounces off in different directions.

If you're throwing a ball, be aware of the enormous size of your Great Dane's mouth and swallowing capacity, so don't choose too small a ball. Instead, opt for a hard soccer ball or better still a football. You can kick or throw either of them a good distance and your Great Dane can carry them easily in his mouth without them deflating.

Mental Stimulation

There seems to be some debate as to just how intelligent Great Danes really are. Many people believe that all dogs are born with basic survival instincts as part of their DNA. Others are of the opinion that intelligence comes from environment, learned behavior, and owner. So if you're convinced that your Great Dane isn't the sharpest tool on the block, you may need to take a peek in the mirror.

Great Danes are inquisitive and curious to the point of being nosy. Due to the strong bonds they form with their owners, your Great Dane will want to know what you're doing and why he isn't involved.

They may be a little clingy at times, but what is curiosity if not a sign of intelligence? Your Great Dane is loyal enough to guard you and your fami-

Photo Courtesy of Taylor Cook

ly with their last breath and are so sensitive that it's possible to reprimand them without even raising your voice. All of which points directly to a high degree of emotional intelligence.

If the potential is there, what can you do to mentally stimulate your Great Dane's gray matter? The easiest way is to take your dog for regular walks. The sights, sounds, and smells of the outside world provide mental stimulus by the bucketful.

This mental stimulation is doubly so for new places. Take him on walks through the forest or on the beach, where he'll go into sniffing overdrive.

While on the subject of sniffing, take advantage of that curious streak (and that huge nose) by playing sniff-out games with your Great Dane. Buy your dog some real stinky treats and hide them around the garden, under boxes in the yard, or throughout the house.

One of the best ways to keep your Great Dane mentally stimulated is to keep his training ongoing by teaching him new tricks and commands. Better still, check out local obedience classes.

Interaction with other dogs is a great brain booster too, so take him to the dog park, where he is going to get a great physical and mental workout.

If the weather is against you then opt for an interactive toy to help mentally stimulate your Great Dane.

Types of Interactive Dog Toys

Electronic Toys: These can stimulate your dog's attention by providing sound and lighting effects

Treat Puzzle Balls: These are usually made of rubber. The ball has chambers which release treats as your dog paws, rolls, and nudges the ball

Snuffle Mats: A snuffle mat is usually made of fleece. Strips of fabric are woven through a robust backing and tied to create hiding spaces on the surface of the mat. Treats are hidden in the hiding spaces for your dog to discover

Frisbees: You can always choose a good old-fashioned Frisbee. They are good for Great Danes as they don't bounce and change course as balls do, so your dog won't need to swerve left and right as they chase it, meaning less risk of playtime injuries. Choose a Frisbee for large dogs that is rugged and durable, rather than the thin plastic variety.

Just make sure that whatever toys you do buy for your Great Dane, you take into account his size and strength—so shop around.

CHAPTER 13
Basic to Advanced Training

"Danes are incredibly versatile. They enjoy activities such as dock div-ing, agility, obedience, lure coursing, fast cat, therapy dog work, barn hunt and more."

Cynthia Neet
Neet Danes

Photo Courtesy of LeighAnn Dodson

Benefits of Training and Your Duty as an Owner

When it comes to Great Danes, the need to have even basic control over this 100-plus-pound animal is essential. The "gentle giant" stereotype is a justifiable description of the breed's predisposition. However, you should never lose sight of the fact that Great Danes are still dogs and, as such, need basic training if they are to be relied upon when faced with new or challenging situations.

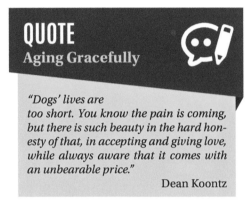

QUOTE
Aging Gracefully

"Dogs' lives are too short. You know the pain is coming, but there is such beauty in the hard honesty of that, in accepting and giving love, while always aware that it comes with an unbearable price."
Dean Koontz

Bringing a Great Dane pup into your life gives you a blank sheet. He doesn't know what to do or when to do it; all he knows is that he wants to please his new family.

For owners taking on adolescent or more mature rescue Great Danes, training can be a slower process, as you may be unaware of the level of training a dog has already experienced. In this case, patience and clear, simple commands are the way to go before advancing to more complex commands.

More than any other breed of dog, a Great Dane needs to feel that its actions are pleasing to a master. The dogs love praise and attention, and in most instances, an adult Great Dane will mope after being reprimanded.

Introducing your dog to even basic commands provides him with the tools to enjoy life to the fullest. Great Danes are intelligent dogs, and by upping the stakes and teaching your dog new and more advanced commands, you will help keep him mentally and physically agile. We will explore both in a later chapter.

This process helps to build stronger bonds between you and your dog and reinforces your status in the relationship.

Setting Realistic Expectations

"Great Danes are very intelligent, but do not like drill sergeant training. They get bored easily, but if you keep training fun for them and rewarding, they learn very fast."

Jackie Herman
Ace-Hi Danes

Being realistic about what to expect from your Great Dane means being patient. Great Danes are equipped with the intelligence to learn, and the fact that they are so eager to please makes training an easier task. This eagerness, coupled with a tendency to be easily distracted, means training must be reinforced continuously.

It is, therefore, important that you set a doable training time frame and consistently stick with the program. You should also set realistic expectations; Great Danes are smart in their own unique way.

Apart from setting realistic goals for your Great Dane, it's also important to have realistic expectations of yourself.

Photo Courtesy of Stacey Ward

Dog Obedience Commands

"Danes are extremely easy to train if you are consistent. Use the same commands and everyone in the household needs to be on the same page. Danes want to please, so if they know the rules, they want to follow them and get the praise."

Carolyn McNamara
Divine Acres Great Danes

Basic Commands

While the majority of Great Dane owners understand the importance of training, very few know where to begin.

There are two basic types of commands: **verbal commands** and **hand signal commands.** You can also train your dog using a whistle.

Hand Signal Commands

For hand signals to be an effective training method, you will first have to teach your dog to frequently look at you. He needs to be able to see the hand signal that corresponds to the verbal command.

Hand signal commands will require a lot of patience. Your dog will not immediately be tuned in to responding. Therefore, a puppy will need facial cues to help him until the hand commands become second nature.

Once your dog has grasped the basics, you will need to phase out the facial and verbal prompts gradually.

Verbal Commands

This method of training is self-explanatory. Verbal commands are your way of communicating to your dog what behavior or action you need from him. They work even when your dog isn't looking directly at you.

Not only can you direct your Great Dane with actual words but also by using a particular tone of voice and volume. Just remember, though, in order not to confuse your dog, it is essential to use the appropriate tone for different types of commands.

Whistle Training

You can use a whistle to give commands, prevent unwanted barking, and to recall your Great Dane. The added benefit of a whistle is that you can use it over long distances. The most important rule to remember is, be consistent with your whistle tones and how they relate to your commands.

You can:

- Adjust the pitch of a whistle to train your Great Dane
- Have different whistles for various commands. For instance, a long whistle could mean "come" while a short whistle could command "sit."

Here, to help you on the road to a well-trained Great Dane, we share some of the most important training commands.

- **Come**

This is one of the most important basic commands to teach your Great Dane.

To teach this command, put your dog on a long leash. Throw a ball and allow him to run after it. Tug gently on the leash while issuing the "come" command. When he returns to you, have a treat ready and waiting. After a short time, you will be able to remove the leash.

- **No**

No treats involved for this command! Most dogs will quickly learn from your tone or facial expression what this command means. For any dogs that resist this, you can also gently tug on the leash to prevent a dog from doing whatever it is you don't want him to do.

Photo Courtesy of Caroline Cannon

Photo Courtesy of
Brittney Anderson

- **Sit**

Teach your puppy or dog this command as soon as possible. Rather than pushing your dog down to force him to sit, walk toward him, lean slightly over him, and issue the command "sit." Your dog will attempt to keep eye contact, causing his head to tilt upward and his rear end to drop to the floor.

- **Lie Down**

Get your Great Dane to sit, then coax him toward the ground by luring him with a treat. Hold the treat one to two feet in front of him at ground level. Once he is lying down, reward him with the treat.

- **Stay**

Begin by commanding your dog to sit. Walk calmly away while keeping eye contact. Continue to issue the command. If your dog attempts to get up, repeat the command to "stay." If your dog follows you, once again command him to "stay." Once he has stopped, command him to "sit" and "stay," then continue slowly walking away. You can practice this over longer distances as your dog progresses.

- **Leave**

This command is vital for your Great Dane's safety. You don't want him picking things up on walks that could be poisonous or harmful to him. The easiest way to teach this command is to choose a dog-friendly food that he doesn't like very much, and train him to ignore it. Drop the item near your dog, and when he pays attention to it, in an appropriate tone of voice, issue the command "leave." Cover the item with your foot or hand, preventing your dog from trying to get to it, and eventually, he will give up.

- **Heel**

Begin by standing with your dog at your leg and facing in the same direction as you. Issue the command "heel" and take two to three steps forward. If your dog follows your pace, reward him with a treat. Continue with this training by building up over longer distances.

- **Wait**

Follow the same teaching method as "leave," but this time aim to get your dog to stop what he is doing until you say it is okay to proceed.

- **Okay**

The command "okay" follows on from "wait." Adopt an appropriate tone and facial expression and tell your dog it is okay to walk on.

- **Release**

Here, you can teach your dog to relax his mouth. The aim is to keep your hand on the object, issuing the command "release" while he releases it to you.

- **Take It**

Hold your dog's favorite toy near his mouth and command him to "take it." When he does, reward him with a treat.

- **Fetch**

Encourage your Great Dane to follow the item you want him to fetch. When he goes for it, reward him with a treat. Take it off him and toss the object again. Issue the command "fetch." When he goes to retrieve it again, give him a treat.

- **Paw or Shake**

Get your dog to give you his paw by issuing the "paw" command. Gently guide his paw to meet your hand. Reward him with a treat each time he does as you ask.

- **Eliminate**

This command does what it says. It tells your dog to pee or defecate on your command. It requires not only a lot of patience but also a little bit of luck, timing-wise. Start by issuing the command when you take your Great Dane for a toilet break. When he goes, repeat the command "eliminate" and give him a treat along with lots of verbal praise.

- **Go**

For this to work, your dog must understand that your verbal cues and hand gestures are referring to a specific location. All you need to do is place a treat in the area, make your dog wait, then point to the place you wish your dog to go where he can enjoy the tasty treat.

- **Catch**

This command is easy, as most dogs love to catch. If yours is a little slow on the uptake, gently throw treats toward his nose while issuing the command "catch." If he doesn't catch the treat quickly in mid-air, pick it up and repeat until he gets the hang of it.

- **Find**

This advanced command is hard to teach unless it is for toys or a treat. Make your Great Dane sit. Show him an item he likes. Have him sit and stay still while you place the item somewhere in the room. Issue the command "find" while pointing at its location. When he goes to the item, give him lots of praise and a treat. You can practice moving the item further away as time goes on, and eventually placing it where he can't see.

- **Hush**

Teaching your dog not to bark unnecessarily is an invaluable skill, and it needs its own command. Saying "no" does not suffice as it not focused enough. Do this when your dog is a puppy by very gently holding his mouth closed while you issue the "hush" command. Note that you should only use this command when necessary, as barking is an integral part of a dog's communication.

Operant Conditioning

"Danes are generally considered to be a 'moderate activity' breed. There is a wide variation within the breed though, with some Danes being true 'couch potatoes' and others being very, very lively and active and energetic."

Barb Bristol
Symmetry Danes

Many believe that American psychologist Edward Thorndike laid the groundwork at the end of the 19th century for operant conditioning (Law of Effect). However, it was many years later in 1938 that B. F. Skinner really nailed it!

Skinner introduced the term "reinforcement." Behavior that is reinforced will be strengthened or repeated, while unenforced behavior will weaken or die out altogether. In other words, if your Great Dane "sits" on command and is rewarded with a treat, he's going to respond to the command again.

To put this into real-world terms, do you think that your Great Dane is more likely to "sit" knowing there's a treat in it, or "sit" because it means you'll stop yelling at him? Exactly, you have it in a nutshell.

The fact that your Great Dane is smart and loves treats and hugs means that it's a win-win for operant conditioning and positive reinforcement every time.

Understanding Primary and Secondary

Reinforcers

Understanding primary and secondary reinforcers will help you gain a clear insight into what motivates your Great Dane to learn.

As the title suggests, reinforced behavior is split into two categories. Let's begin with the first.

Primary Reinforcers

These tap into the rudimentary operating instructions imbedded in your Great Dane's DNA. They cover a dog's basic survival needs such as food and water.

A good example of this is when you're training your dog to "sit." On successful completion of the task, you reward him with a treat. The repetition of the command and subsequent treat helps your dog to learn and remember. The awarding of the treat taps into his primary need for food.

Secondary (or Conditioned) Reinforcers

These come into play when you stimulate interest by introducing an incentive or an action that reinforces its connection to a primary reinforcer.

As the basic commands when training your Great Dane are so important, the use of a treat confirms in his brain that obeying an instruction means food, and food makes your dog happy.

Because we want to save treats as a reward for the most important commands, we have to bring in secondary reinforcement. So when you're teaching your Great Dane to fetch a ball or stick, his reward for retrieval is praise and an ear rub.

He will then associate the retrieval of a stick with praise. Praise makes him happy, and he associates the feeling of happiness with a treat. So although he doesn't get a treat, which is a primary reinforcer, he associates it with the secondary reinforcer (praise).

Dog behaviorists theorize that as praise isn't a primary survival need for a dog, you are therefore conditioning your dog to respond to a secondary stimulus.

In my experience, when it comes to Great Danes, praise and ear rubbing are so fundamental to their well-being that they should be elevated to primary status.

Understanding Negative Reinforcement Dangers

"For their massive size they are actually very sensitive and can have their feelings hurt very easily. Then tend to be what we call soft as far as training and only succeed with positive reward based training."

Brandy Massey
Massey Great Danes

Many people see the term "negative reinforcement training" and believe that it involves using undesirable or harmful methods to train your dog. Many owners question whether or not it should it be part of a dog's training at all.

In training terms, if positive reinforcement is giving something (like a treat) as a reward for an action, then negative reinforcement means taking something away in relation to a command.

For example, when teaching your Great Dane to "sit," you give the command and then physically push his back end down, only removing your hand when he is sitting. From this point on, touching his rear is the signal to sit, and when he feels your hand taken away, he sees that as the task being complete.

The removal of your hand, in this case, is a negative reinforcement. This method can also be used to curb bad behavior.

Say, for instance, your Great Dane frequently jumps up, seeking your attention. By not giving him the response he wants, i.e., head rubs and encouragement, you're taking away your attention. This action means that when he realizes jumping up gets him nowhere, he will no longer do it.

Negative reinforcement is not for everyone and, used incorrectly or in the wrong circumstances, can be detrimental to your dog's training regime. Take, for example, feeding time; to ensure your dog doesn't become aggressive, conventional methods suggest removing his food mid-meal, then replacing it right away.

This method shows him that although you gave it to him, you can also take it away too. Taking it away is using negative reinforcement to let him know who's boss. Do it too often, however, or for no specific reason, and your Great Dane may associate you being near his food bowl with a loss of food. This can result in aggressive food guarding.

Round-Up of Alternative Training Methods

There are lots of alternative dog training methods used today, and it can be confusing to you as an owner. The best way forward is to discover which one suits both you and your Great Dane.

Here are four alternative training methods to consider:

- Electronic Training

- Mirror Training

- Dominance

- Relationship-Based Training

Electronic Training

This training method is controversial and, according to some canine behaviorists, can negatively impact your dog due to the fact that you are training through a punishment method. Before we say why, though, let's look at what it involves.

Electronic training generally refers to an electronic device attached to the dog's collar that, when activated by the owner, delivers an electric shock or buzzing sensation that can be increased in increments.

E-collars, as they are better known, are primarily used off-leash or for distance training. For instance, if your property has no physical boundary or if you need to train your dog to respond when running free, e-collars might be a consideration.

The collar can be regulated for automatic activation if the dog passes a certain marker or is owner-activated by way of a handheld remote. Depending on the type of e-collar, it is possible to increase the intensity and duration of the shock.

Scent and Bark Collars

Some owners prefer to use scent or bark collars, which operate along similar lines but produce a vaporized spray of citronella under the dog's chin. An audio device in the collar detects the bark and issues the spray, which dogs may find irritating.

As you can imagine, some dog owners would rather wear the shock collar themselves than hang it around the neck of their beloved Great Dane. However, some professional dog trainers believe that in the right hands, the e-collar is an extremely useful tool, especially for working dogs.

"In the right hands,' is the key factor here. Improper, disproportionate strength of the shock or overuse can lead to your dog's suffering not only from the physical shock but also psychologically from negative imprinting.

By comparison, citronella collars may be considered more humane. This essential oil derives from lemongrass, and in the tiny quantities used in such collars, is annoying rather than harmful to dogs.

Citronella is also used to deter mosquitoes, so a bark-collar may also have a positive role for dog owners in high mosquito areas. Be aware, though, that as the collar's intended use is as a bark deterrent, the dog is punished for an action and is, therefore, responding to negative reinforcement.

Exposing your Great Dane to too much citronella is not a good thing either. Excessive barking can result in too much of the product getting into his eyes and mouth.

Mirror Training

Mirror training takes advantage of your Great Dane's ability to learn through observation. Its name comes from the fact that you, as the trainer, teach your Great Dane by encouraging him to mimic or copy your actions.

If you sit down on the floor, your Great Dane will copy you. A Great Dane will want to please its owner and will therefore mirror your actions.

This method is perfect for the Great Dane breed as they are very inquisitive and will have no trouble standing by your side watching the process.

This method is most successful for owners who enjoy a particularly good bond with their dog, and it also encourages positive reinforcement.

Dominance

This method taps into your Great Dane's pack mentality and places you as the human Alpha in the relationship. This method is viable for one dog or more and assumes your Great Dane will naturally take the role of canine Alpha of his small pack.

To establish dominance, you have to use such techniques as making your dog sit for food, sit calmly before going outside, wait for you to enter or leave a room first, and walk to heel on a leash.

To reinforce your role as the dominant, it is advisable not to allow your Great Dane to sit on the sofa with you or lie on your bed.

Bending down to your dog's eye level is also a no-no with this training method as this tells him he is your equal.

Photo Courtesy of
Megan Jones

Dominance training does not mean yelling and screaming at your Great Dane either, merely adopting an authoritative tone when issuing a command.

Relationship-Based Training

Relationship-based training is more of a holistic approach which helps the relationship between you and your dog evolve over time. This bonding allows an owner to understand what makes a Great Dane tick. It also highlights the stimuli a dog most readily reacts to along with any triggers that will impact negatively on him.

The progression of this method will see the owner correctly decipher his dog's body language. It will provide an indication as to when he is stressed, happy, or weary, allowing your actions or commands to be more in tune.

As time goes on you will gradually become more intuitive, understanding why certain commands appear to fall on deaf ears or which circumstances create a perfect learning environment for your dog.

Relationship-based training isn't for everyone, as it requires even more time and patience than usual. It is dictated by how you are with your dog and what kind of relationship you want to share with him.

Owners who choose this path are rewarded with the type of unbreakable bond that takes Great Dane ownership to the next level.

Dog Training Obedience Classes

"Puppy obedience classes are a must for every new Dane owner to teach you confidence in your ability to handle your dog. If you have confidence in yourself, your puppy will have confidence in you and accept you as their leader."

Janie Pronto
Nuttree Great Danes

There is a whole host of reasons as to why you may decide you need help with obedience training your dog, from being unable to commit to the training schedule due to work and personal commitments, to falling short of initial expectations.

In opting for a dog training class, you're not handing over the reins or throwing in the proverbial towel. Instead, you are taking responsibility for your Great Dane's well-being.

How to Choose a Suitable Dog Training Obedience Class

A dog training class should be hosted by a professional and experienced trainer. It isn't just about teaching your Great Dane basic commands. A class is also a great way to boost your dog's confidence and enhance your relationship with him. Thus, it's very important to choose the right class and host for your particular dog.

Where you live and how far you are prepared to travel to a class will have an impact on how many options are available to you. The best place to begin your search is by locating and contacting a trusted dog rescue shelter or by asking your veterinarian for recommendations.

You can also search for accredited dog trainers or local classes online. Contact a class leader and ask if it is possible to chat with them first or even observe one of their sessions before committing and paying class fees.

If you are looking to arrange one-on-one private training, rather than a group class, follow the same guidelines.

At the end of the day, a dog training class is a positive tool that brings with it a whole host of benefits for you and your Great Dane.

Types of Classes

• Beginner Classes
If your Great Dane is new to you or has little or no training, opt for a beginner class. Here, you can expect to learn the basics of:

Sit

Down

Stay

Leave

Recall and Leash Training

• Intermediate Classes
These classes are aimed at dogs who have learned the basics and are ready to move on and build on the skills already mastered. You may, however, be asked to complete a Beginners Class before moving up to Intermediate Level.

- **Specialty or Advanced Classes**

The type of class you join will depend on your Great Dane's individual needs. For example, is he lunging or barking at other dogs? Is he fearful around new experiences? Or do you just want to keep him mentally stimulated by teaching him advanced tricks? Again, by doing a little research (as above), you can find the class that is right for you and your dog.

CHAPTER 14
Dealing with Unacceptable Behavior

Breed-Specific Bad Habits

"A Great Dane can quickly realize that it is becoming large enough to reach you face, the place where all the talking and love comes from. They will inherently, at some point, feel like jumping up to greet you is a brilliant idea. It is our job to make this very unpleasant. Using a short and strong 'off' command in this moment, sometimes coupled with turning around, has always made it very clear to the dog that this is an unwanted behavior."

Nathan Bolby
Grand Mimeux

*Photo Courtesy of
Kim Gramling*

By nature, Great Danes are easygoing, even-tempered, and mild-mannered. If trained from an early age, they will be well behaved and loving canine companions.

They do have some breed-specific bad habits that may, at times, be troublesome. The majority of these can be avoided via basic training.

Bad habits include:

- Puppies can be rowdy and overenthusiastic, causing damage inside the house and out

- Adult and puppy Great Danes tend to suffer from separation anxiety, and this can lead to destructiveness if they are left alone for long periods

- This giant breed of dog is both heavy and affectionate, and you will sometimes have to deal with 100-plus pounds of weight leaning against your leg or attempting to sit on your lap

- A Great Dane needs constant companionship in order to prevent him from becoming depressed

- These are strong-willed dogs and need a confident owner

- Great Danes are exuberant greeters. This often results in them jumping up on you, your family, and your guests. Some Great Danes may be aggressive or dominant to other family pets of the same sex

- Great Danes are a restless breed, and when they are inside, they want to go out, and when out, they want to come back indoors!

- Great Danes may chase and grab small fleeing animals, including cats

- Great Danes that are fearful can defensively bite if cornered

- The majority of Great Danes are stand-offish with strangers

- This giant breed loves to paw the ground or floor surfaces. Their huge paws can cause a lot of damage

The important thing to remember is that what is cute behavior in a Yorkshire Terrier is cause for concern in a Great Dane! So nip any bad behavior in the bud as soon as possible.

Identify and Dealing with Unwanted Behavior

From time to time, your perfect dog will do something that you deem unacceptable. Regardless of whether your Great Dane is chewing your favorite slippers or ripping up the mail, your first reaction may be to yell "no."

However, as most professional dog trainers will tell you, this two-letter word is not the one to use in instances such as these.

Why? Because it gives your Great Dane no direction of what you want him to do and shouting at him can go a long way toward damaging your relationship with him.

So how do you stop this unwanted behavior?

Management, aka Prevention

You must make sure your Great Dane no longer has the chance to "practice" the bad behavior that needs to stop. To do this, you need to prevent your dog from being able to carry out the undesirable behavior in the first place.

For instance, if your Great Dane is a chewer, put clothes and shoes away. If your dog rushes to the front door, consider installing a child or dog gate.

Prevention is the name of the game here.

Remove Reinforcement

A dog will do what a dog will do. He may be anxious or stressed and exhibit behavior that is unacceptable to humans. He may think it's fun to jump up, or bark, or rip up socks.

So try and find out what makes your dog tick. Is his jumping up attention seeking? Does he chew your clothes because he is bored? Does pulling on his leash mean he gets to go where he wants? For instance, my senior Great Dane, Jax Teller, incessantly barks at 5 p.m. every day, meaning he thinks it's time for dinner!

Photo Courtesy of
Brianna Montano

To prevent unwanted behavior, you have to get to the source of the problem and either remove it or meet a dog's needs in an alternative and positive way.

Provide an Alternative

Teach your Great Dane to replace the bad behavior with good. You need to decide what you would like your dog to do instead of the bad behavior. For example:

- Rather than jumping up on me when I arrive home, I would like my Great Dane to wait calmly

- Rather than barking incessantly for his dinner, I would like my dog to calmly come and remind me it's time to eat

- Rather than pulling on the leash when we are out walking, I would like my Great Dane to walk alongside me

And so on, until you devise a way of giving your dog something to do in place of the unwanted behavior.

Positive Interrupters (Cue Words)

If your dog is doing something that is either unsafe or irritating, you must put an end to it. The important thing here is how.

For instance, if you see that your Great Dane is about to try and jump on your lap and you don't want him to, calmly and consistently interrupt him.

Next, redirect him to his own space. In other words, make him stop whatever he is doing and ensure he pays attention to you.

You can do this by choosing a noise or word, maybe a click of the tongue or the command "leave." The word you use is irrelevant; it's the tone of voice that matters.

You want your dog to identify this as his cue, so use a happy tone rather than a threatening one. Now you see why the word "no" isn't applicable, as it tends to have negative connotations.

Issue your cue word and give your dog his favorite treat. Speak your chosen word in an upbeat tone and feed him several treats in quick succession until he looks joyfully toward you when he hears his positive interrupter (cue word).

Disengage and Pay Attention

Say the cue word to your Great Dane when he is slightly distracted. He should look at you happily, awaiting his special treats. When this happens, mark the moment and say "yes." Give him more of his favorite treats, again one after the other. Repeat the process until he is happy and starting to engage with you every time he hears the cue word.

Distract and Redirect

Begin with simple distractions and slowly work your way upward to more challenging ones. For instance, if your dog gets hold of a towel, use your cue word to interrupt him and encourage him to chew a toy in its place. Remember, while an interruption will work at the time, it won't always teach your Great Dane not to repeat the bad behavior in the future.

Time for Timeout

If your puppy nips you while playing, you can "mark" the moment he hurts you by saying "ouch" and stopping play for 5-10 seconds. Return to play once more, stopping should the nipping continue. He will eventually switch to gently mouthing in order to keep the playtime going.

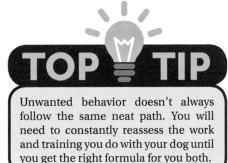

Unwanted behavior doesn't always follow the same neat path. You will need to constantly reassess the work and training you do with your dog until you get the right formula for you both.

The key to this technique is all in the timing. You have to make it crystal clear to your Great Dane what behavior is responsible for causing the fun to stop. So use this technique carefully and sparingly.

The Role of an Animal Behaviorist

Despite your obedience training efforts, does your Great Dane jump up on visitors or destroy the cushions on the sofa? If the answer is yes, then you may need an animal behaviorist rather than a dog trainer.

Unlike a dog trainer, an animal behaviorist is required to have a bachelor's degree.

A behaviorist delves far deeper into your dog's behavior and is more knowledgeable regarding emotions, neuroscience, and the scientific and objective study of animal behavior (ethology).

More often than not, a behaviorist will be an experienced dog handler with a good deal of hands-on, practical experience along with a degree level of formal training.

Not only will they identify your Great Dane's problematic behavior, but they will also devise a customized action and follow-up plan to help you get your buddy back on track.

Look for a professional that is certified with a recognized organization. You can do this with online research or by chatting with your local veterinary practice or even via networking with other Great Dane owners.

CHAPTER 15
Basic Health Care

Vet Visits

Get your Great Dane used to visiting the veterinarian when he is well. Dogs who only visit the vet when they are ill or injured are more likely to be anxious or stressed.

Popping into the practice once in a while for a chat is also a great way to associate a vet visit with a positive feeling.

Photo Courtesy of
Kathy Jerding

Scheduled Check-Ups

Even if your Great Dane is fighting fit and has no health issues, it is important to schedule annual check-ups with your veterinarian. If your dog is a senior or has specific medical needs, aim for more frequent check-ups.

A check-up gives your vet the opportunity to highlight any potential health issues and deal with them before they become a problem. As your veterinarian becomes more familiar with your Great Dane, it gives them an ideal opportunity to identify small changes in your dog's overall health, too.

Your vet may begin the check-up appointment by asking you about your Great Dane's eating and drinking habits, his stools, and overall general health.

A head-to-toe check-up with your vet could include:

- Weighing your dog
- Examining your Great Dane's joints, paws, legs, and reproductive organs
- Monitoring his lungs and heart
- Checking his coat, skin, eyes, ears, teeth, and mouth
- Externally examining his abdomen for any irregular signs

- Scanning his microchip to make sure that it is readable and in the correct position. Occasionally microchips can migrate which means they can be missed when someone carries out a scan
- Making sure your dog's vaccinations are up to date
- Senior dogs or those with specific health issues may need diagnostic screening. These could include blood tests, X-rays, heart worm testing, etc.
- Updating your Great Dane's vaccination records

A scheduled check-up is also a good time to discuss any concerns you may have about your dog's overall health.

Vaccinations, Neutering, Fleas, Ticks, and Worms

Vaccinations

Although making sure that your Great Dane's vaccinations are up to date will be a part of his regular check-up, if these do not tie in with your appointment, your vet will likely send you a reminder.

Timings will depend on which vaccination is due but may include Kennel Cough (Bordetella), Parvovirus, Adenovirus, Distemper, Leptorspirosis,

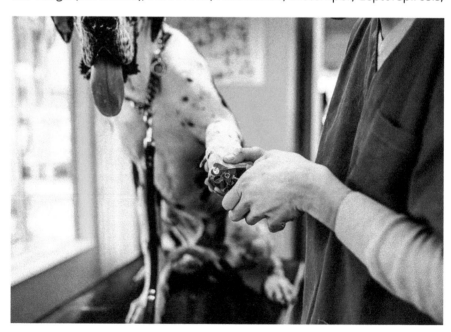

Photo Courtesy of
Georgia Nicholson

and Parainfluenza. For anyone planning to take their Great Dane overseas, a Rabies vaccination is also necessary.

Neutering

Neutering is a form of sterilization which is carried out under general anesthesia. In most cases, it is recommended for dogs over the age of six months.

You may have adopted a rescue dog that is already neutered. However, if this is not the case, and you have either an un-neutered adult dog or puppy, neutering is something that should be considered.

There are many pro and cons to neutering your dog, and these include:

Photo Courtesy of Ellie Hoffmann

Pros

- Neutered male dogs have a decreased risk of contracting prostate cancer and for female dogs, spaying means no threat of ovarian cancer. It also reduces the risk of breast cancer

- Testicle removal will reduce your male dog's desire to spray and mark his territory

- Neutering can stabilize your male dog's mood, making him less aggressive over time

- Neutering will reduce your Great Dane's urge to mate, mount other dogs, or leg-hump humans

- Spaying your female dog will result in less mess as there will be no bloody discharge

Cons

- Behavioral changes are not guaranteed

- Neutering and spaying may cause incontinence

- The texture of your Great Dane's coat may alter due to the hormone changes

- Dogs that are neutered before they are one year old have an increased risk of different health issues. Talk to your vet about this as it will depend on your dog's gender and history

- The operation is irreversible so you will no longer be able to breed your Great Dane

Not all dogs benefit from neutering, so talk to your veterinarian about the whole process. At the end of the day, the choice is yours.

Fleas, Tick, and Worming Treatments

This is a subject where prevention is 100 percent better than cure.

Flea larvae can live in the home and garden all year round. Ticks can transmit very nasty diseases, and worms can affect the overall health of your Great Dane.

Fleas and Ticks

When to treat your Great Dane with flea and tick products will depend very much on where you are living.

While fleas are always around, they are at their worst in warm weather. Ticks can live all year round in some climates but are more prevalent in spring and summer. Speak to your vet about what is needed and when.

Check with Your Vet

Before you buy over-the-counter flea and tick products, speak with your vet if your dog is:

- Taking other medications

- Senior or ill

- A puppy

- Pregnant or nursing
- Allergic to flea and tick products

In any of the above cases, your veterinarian may suggest you buy a dog-specific flea comb to pick up fleas, ticks, and eggs. If you do go down this route, remember to wear disposable gloves and always wash your hands in soap and water afterwards.

Safety Advice: Don't ever double up on treatments. For instance, don't use both a spot-on product along with a powder. Always follow the package directions and never use a cat product on a dog, and vice versa. Some flea collars are lethal to cats and dogs so always purchase them from your vet rather than a store.

Worming

The thought of a worm wriggling inside your Great Dane's body is enough to make you squirm with horror.

Combine this with the possibility that dog worms can cause illness in both pets and humans, and you have a nightmare scenario.

Your Great Dane can get worms in a number of ways:

- An infected female dog may pass them on to her puppies either before they are born or through her milk
- Your dog may contract them by eating worm-infected animal feces
- Your dog may contract them by eating mice or rats that are infected with roundworm eggs

These are some of the tell-tale signs that your Great Dane has worms:

- Worms or eggs that are visible in their feces
- Worms or eggs that are visible in the rear-end and the surrounding fur
- Your dog is rubbing or scratching his bottom
- Worms in vomit
- Bloated belly or stomach
- Bloody diarrhea
- Weight loss, increased appetite, and constant hunger which results in weight loss

Worms

The most common types of worms in dogs are:

- **Heartworms:** Heartworms can result in severe problems with the heart, lungs, kidneys, and liver. Their larvae are transmitted via infected mosquitoes. This particular type of worm can lead to death. Heartworms can also be painful and expensive to treat.

- **Hookworms:** Short, blood-sucking parasites with teeth. They strip nutrients from puppies which means they can be fatal. While they are uncommon in UK, they can be found in the US and Europe.

- **Roundworms:** There are two types of roundworms that can affect dogs. They are toxascaris leonine and toxocara canis. Both species are long, white, and have a spaghetti-like appearance. They absorb nutrients from the affected animal.

- **Tapeworms:** This type of worm is flat and long. They can be over six inches in length. Unless your dog is very active, they won't harm your pet as there are lots of nutrients for both the worm and the host. When excreted in the feces, they split into small, grain-of-rice-like segments

- **Whipworms:** This type of worm rarely poses any problems for dogs as they live in the large intestine and extract a lot less nutrients than other types of parasites

Treatment of Worms

If left untreated worms can result in health complications. To prevent the spreading of worms, always pick up and responsibly dispose of your pet's feces as soon as possible.

There are a number of effective and safe de-worming medications, and your vet will advise which one is right for you.

Your dog will need between one and three initial doses to kill the worms, along with a follow-up dose to kill any new worms.

Many vets de-worm puppies at around two to three weeks old.

Tail Docking and Ear Cropping Explained

Great Danes are born with a long, whippy tail and soft, floppy ears.

So, why in the United States do you see so many Great Danes with pointed, cropped ears and a docked tail?

Photo Courtesy of Hayley Johnson

• Tail Docking

Not only is a Great Dane's tail super long, but it is also very powerful. By nature, these giant dogs are happy and wag their tail a lot, whacking everything it comes into contact with.

It hurts a lot if you get smacked and can cause all sorts of damage to your furniture, not to mention result in a bloody, sore tail and subsequent tail trauma. In extreme cases, amputation may be necessary to prevent further damage to the tail.

Cautionary Tail! Our senior Great Dane, Jax Teller, once wagged his happy tail so vigorously against a tree trunk, he knocked the tip off. It took weeks to heal and was very painful.

• Ear Cropping

Once upon a time, Great Danes' ears were cropped to prevent them from tearing or ripping during a boar hunt.

Today, ear cropping is performed mainly for cosmetic purposes. The procedure is carried out at around six to eight weeks.

While in the US, Great Dane ear cropping is a common sight for all show dogs, it is frowned upon in many other parts of the world unless for medical reasons.

Both surgeries are unnecessary and are largely driven by the wish to follow a breed standard and aesthetic, so speak to your vet for further advice.

Holistic Alternatives

You can help your Great Dane by combining conventional medicine and treatments with holistic care.

Perhaps your dog is recovering from surgery. While medication can help prevent infection and disease, a holistic treatment such as massage can help to ease your dog's pain and encourage the healing process.

Here are some of the most popular holistic treatments available to your Great Dane.

Canine Acupuncture

Using needles to stimulate the human body's pressure points has been practiced for thousands of years.

In 1988, canine acupuncture became an approved alternate therapy by the American Veterinary Medical Association.

Today, it is used for dogs to relieve muscle and joint pain, encourage healing after surgery or trauma and, in some cases, to treat the symptoms of diseases such as cancer and diabetes.

Canine acupuncture hardly has any side effects and does not interfere with medications or other treatments, but can be costly and requires multiple sessions.

Speak to your vet and ask if this alternative treatment is right for your Great Dane.

Canine Massage

Many dog owners believe that this treatment improves and encourages nerve stimulation and blood flow, relaxes muscles, and relieves stress.

The jury is out as to how effective a treatment it is for your dog. However, if it feels good, do it! And doesn't your Great Dane deserve a soothing massage?

Giving your dog a regular rubdown will help you check him for lumps or sore spots too. If you find any, consult your vet at once as massage can worsen pain and swelling.

Alternatively, get Googling and treat your dog to his own personal, albeit costly, professional canine massage therapist.

Chinese Herbal Medicine

Supporters of herbal medicine for canines believe it is useful in relieving pain, restoring or improving organ function, and supporting and strengthening the immune system.

While many dog owners claim an improvement in their pet's health from using this method of treatment, the benefits are not medically proven.

Some herbs are not safe to use alongside other medications and can cause diarrhea and vomiting. It's a good idea, therefore, to ask your vet for their opinion on the use of herbal treatments.

Chiropractic Treatment

Chiropractors manipulate the musculoskeletal system. They do this using gentle, fast motions to help restore movement or improve joint function and relieve pressure on the surrounding tissue.

While there is no scientific explanation as to exactly why or how this works, it is often used successfully to treat a number of canine problems, including upset stomachs and arthritis.

Hydrotherapy

Physical water therapy is ideal for Great Danes needing low-impact exercise. If your dog is suffering from arthritis, joint pain, is in recovery after an injury or accident, or is overweight or elderly, this safe cardiovascular treatment could be the one for him.

Hydrotherapy is not only a good, gentle workout, but it can also help improve mobility, build muscle, decrease stress, and increase circulation.

Your Great Dane can enjoy the heated water of a pool where he will swim or walk using an underwater treadmill.

Depending on how much your Great Dane loves water, he may need to wear a life jacket or harness to help keep him above the water level.

Magnetic Field Therapy

Magnet therapy is the use of magnetic fields to treat injury or illness. It is most often used to enhance wound healing and to treat connective tissue and chronic joint pain conditions.

It is inexpensive, has hardly any side effects, and is non-invasive.

Many pet owners are huge fans of this treatment, but it remains unpopular amongst the medical profession.

If you are interested in learning more, chat with your veterinarian about the possibility of magnet therapy in conjunction with medical treatment.

While none of these holistic treatments are scientifically proven, for the main part, they have no adverse side effects.

Let your Great Dane guide you with his energy levels, mood, and response.

If in any doubt, consult a holistic vet who uses alternative treatments in conjunction with proven Western medicine.

Choosing Pet Insurance

Owning any dog is a responsibility, and this is never more so than in the case of a Great Dane.

Great Danes are susceptible to a number of serious and ongoing illnesses, and it is important, therefore, to consider taking out a comprehensive insurance policy.

Hopefully, you will never have to make an insurance claim. However, why not sleep peacefully at night, knowing that if the worst happens, your dog will have access to the medical care and treatment he needs and deserves?

Bloat, Hip Dysplasia, Elbow Dysplasia, and **Hypothyroidism** are just four of the most common Great Dane conditions and diseases resulting in insurance claims.

Bloat is the number one cause of Great Dane death. The key to treating bloat is prompt emergency treatment. This treatment is costly, and depending on the level of care needed, can run into the thousands of dollars.

Hip Dysplasia is mainly an inherited condition. It can, however, according to new evidence, be caused by too rapid a growth during the first 12 months of a Great Dane puppy's life. Over time it can result in pain, difficulty walking, arthritis, and even lameness or paralysis. Surgeries to help correct this issue can be as much as $4,000+.

Elbow Dysplasia is similar to Hip Dysplasia, but here, the malformed elbow joint leads to the destruction of surrounding tissue, wear and tear, and, finally, osteoarthritis. The necessary surgery can be several thousand dollars.

Hypothyroidism is a disease that can affect Great Danes of any age but often develops between one to three years of age. It is possible to treat it with diet and medication. However, testing is necessary to diagnose the condition, and this can cost anywhere from a couple hundred dollars up to $1,000+.

Pet insurance is a sensible plan for helping you to meet your Great Dane's veterinary costs.

There are a vast number of companies offering canine insurance plans and you will need to research the best one to suit your budget and needs. You can do this by chatting with your vet, researching online, talking to your breeder, or networking with other dog owners.

Once you have found a plan you think may be suitable, make a list of the questions you should ask prospective insurers.

- In the event of a claim, can I choose my veterinarian?

- Are there any exclusions? Some plans exclude preexisting medical conditions, so find out at the outset what is and what isn't covered by your plan
- Does the plan cover routine checks, vaccines, testing, and dental issues?
- Is spaying or neutering covered by this insurance?
- Does this insurance plan cover prescription charges?
- Am I liable to pay a deductible, and if so, what are the limits?
- Are there any incident or illness caps?

It is important to feel comfortable with the insurance provider you choose. They will be handling any future claims you make, and depending on the nature of the claim, this can be an upsetting or trying time.

How they handle your initial questions is a good indication as to their level of customer service, so don't be afraid to ask.

Finally, make sure the company you choose to go with is reputable. You can do this by researching reviews from other Great Dane owners and speaking with them about the plans they use and their experience with claims they have made.

Personal Experience

As a young adult, Jax Teller once ate a selection of laundry. The result of this was a costly operation to remove the offending items from his intestine. The cost ran into the thousands.

This happened less than 48 hours before my family and I were due to fly to Spain for a Christmas vacation.

While the insurance covered Jax's vet bills, hospitalization, and after-care, it would not cover the cancellation of our flights or accommodations.

According to the insurance company, because we had taken him to the vet 10 days prior to the emergency (due to a bout of diarrhea), we were unable to add this to our claim. They said this decision was based on their belief that this was an ongoing stomach-related problem.

The two issues were unrelated, and our vet argued with the company to confirm this too. Even though our expensive, all-singing, all-dancing insurance policy did include holiday cancellation compensation as a result of emergency vet treatment, they refused to compensate us.

So my advice is, read the small print.

CHAPTER 16
Senior Dog Health and Care

Common Health Problems in Senior Danes

Regardless of their size, we like to think that our loving and gentle Great Dane will remain eternally young.

Unfortunately, this isn't the case. Luckily, you can help to improve and maybe even extend your dog's life. You can do this by making yourself aware of some of the common health problems he may experience as he enters his senior years.

Giant breeds age a lot quicker than small-size dogs. A Great Dane, whose life span is shorter than most, may begin to show signs of age-related health issues a lot earlier than the norm.

Here are some common health problems to look out for in your senior Great Dane.

Photo Courtesy of Cassie Heidmann

Cancer

Your dog's lumps and bumps are not all cancerous. However, there is an increased risk of cancer in older dogs, so get them checked out by your vet.

HELPFUL TIP

With a life span of 7-10 years, Great Dane "Golden Years" approach quickly. Some Danes decline rapidly as they age, while others grow old elegantly. All dog owners, regardless of the breed, should treat their dogs with compassion and advocate on their behalf.

Dementia

Your senior dog may appear confused, disorientated, or bark and whine for no reason. He may appear to be lost in his usually familiar surroundings or stare into space for long periods of time. While there is no cure for dementia, it can be helped with medication and diet. These are symptoms that may also be an indication of other conditions, so have a chat with your vet if you notice any of these behaviors.

Gastrointestinal Issues (GI) and Incontinence

GI issues can be the cause of any number of problems in a senior dog. Not all are they serious, but they can indicate health problems such as kidney disease. If your Great Dane has a bout of diarrhea or vomiting that doesn't quickly clear up, contact your vet.

Incontinence can be an indicator of dementia or loss of bladder control. Again, speak with your veterinarian.

Heart Problems

As dogs age, they can develop heart disease. Signs of possible heart disease include unexplained vomiting, an intolerance to exercise, loss of consciousness, and difficulty breathing.

Joint Problems

The most common cause of joint pain and stiffness in senior dogs is osteoarthritis. It is a progressive and degenerative disease that causes the loss of lubrication and wearing away of cartilage in the hips, leg joints, and shoulders. While no cure exists, there are pain-reducing treatments available. It is important to make sure your senior dog has a nutrient-rich dog food to help maintain his joints.

Kidney Issues

As your Great Dane ages, his kidney function will suffer. Chronic kidney failure is incurable, but with the correct treatment, it can be managed. Routine blood tests can identify the disease in its early stages, so make sure your senior dog is checked out by the vet every six months. Nutrition is also an important factor in keeping your dog's kidneys healthy, so once again, speak with your vet about any concerns you may have.

Photo Courtesy of
Rebecca Drewek

Loss of Hearing and Vision

Tissue degeneration in the ears and eyes can cause your senior dog to become (in varying degrees) deaf, blind, or both. Your Great Dane may also develop cataracts. These are a cloudy layer that forms over the lens of the eye, causing, at best, partial blindness and, at worst, complete blindness. As dogs rely heavily on their sense of smell, this may not cause your dog too much trouble. In some cases, it may be possible for cataracts to be surgically removed. Hearing loss, on the other hand, is permanent. So on a regular basis, clean and care for your Great Dane's ears. This simple regime may help to slow down the progression of your dog's hearing loss as he enters his twilight years.

Discuss with your vet any problems that concern you, no matter how big or small. If your practice is concerned, they may suggest a urine or blood sample to check for underlying issues.

Talk to him about your dog's appetite too, as there are many problems which can be simply managed though a change of diet.

Illness and Injury Prevention

"The top causes of death in Danes are heart disease, cancer and bloat. We have a health clearance test for heart disease but don't yet have a predictive one. There is a genetic test for bloat, but there are also non-genetic causes of that disease. It is possible for these conditions to 'lurk' in a pedigree and even the most responsible breeder won't be aware of it."

Barb Bristol
Symmetry Danes

Keeping your senior Great Dane free from illness and injury is not as challenging as it may sound. It takes only a few simple changes to your dog's living space and lifestyle to ensure that he is happy and healthy for a long time to come.

Weight Watching

Being overweight, or worse still, obese, can decrease your dog's life expectancy. Thankfully, it is one of the simplest things to monitor and control.

If you feel your senior dog has packed on the pounds due to his metabolic rate slowing down and is less active than he used to be, you may need to consider, under the advice of your vet, changing your Great Dane's diet, reassessing his exercise regime, or even reducing the amount he eats.

Your vet may suggest your dog is given a specialized diet or has vitamins and minerals to supplement his food.

If your Great Dane is flatulent, you may need to add more fiber to his diet.

On the flip side, if your dog is eating less than usual, it may be a sign of dental problems.

If in doubt, you guessed it; make an appointment with your local vet.

Photo Courtesy of
Caz Brown

Exercise for Mind, Body, and Soul

As far as exercise is concerned, to prevent injury, it may be a good idea to slow down your dog's regular regime. Switch from running to walking and consider swimming. It's the perfect way to keep your dog fit and healthy without placing pressure on those all-important senior joints.

Mobility exercises, such as walking up and down steps, are a good way to promote positive movement too. Arrange play dates with other senior dogs in a controlled environment such as your garden or yard.

Mental stimulation will help to keep your dog's mind healthy, so use puzzles and chews. These not only promote mental stimulation but are also a useful way of burning off those unwanted calories.

To help him remain free from injury, reduce the intensity of your senior Great Dane's exercise while making sure he is happy and healthy.

Sleep

Senior dogs also have more specific sleep requirements. They sleep a lot more than younger dogs, so make sure that sleep time is comfortable and relaxing.

You can do this by:

- Making sure that sleeping areas, both inside and out, are draft free
- Providing cozy, warm blankets for them to rest on
- Purchasing suitable coats for outdoor walking or playing
- Discouraging your dog from lying on hard floors such as tiles, concrete, and wooden floorboards

Final Thoughts

If your senior dog is suffering from loss of vision, why not rearrange the furniture so that it is against the walls rather than in the middle of the room? Remember, you will need to teach him the new layout. You can do this by walking your dog around the new layout while on a leash two to three times a day until he is comfortable.

Also, consider child gates to prevent your dog from falling downstairs, cushion sharp corners, and make sure swimming pools, fireplaces, and other dangerous areas are blocked off.

Warning Signs That It May Be Time to Say Goodbye

Sometimes it's a crystal-clear decision. Your Great Dane may be injured, in severe pain and discomfort, or so elderly that the only option is to let him cross over the Rainbow Bridge.

One thing is for sure, though, the final decision to euthanize your dog, who is a valued part of your family dynamic, is not one to be taken lightly.

While you may know in your heart that the time has come to say goodbye, here are 15 warning signs to help you make that difficult decision.

- Has your Great Dane's appetite for food and water decreased? Lack of appetite is often an indication of pain

- Extreme weight loss. The majority of dogs will be weighed during their annual check-up, which means gradual weight loss is difficult to identify. Weight loss doesn't happen overnight, however you may suddenly notice one day how thin your dog has become. This problem could be a case of lack of appetite or your dog's body being unable to process nutrients

- Does your dog excessively gnaw, chew, or lick a problem area such as an existing injury or wound?

Photo Courtesy of
Zach and Megan Williams

- Is your dog limping or yelping when walking or going up and down stairs?

- Does your dog's temperament seem different, such as snapping at children and adults or growling at other animals? Mood changes are a sign of depression

- Have you noticed your Great Dane withdrawing from life? Many behaviorists say that a dog knows when it's time to die and will isolate himself in an attempt not to slow down the pack or cause trauma to loved ones. Your dog may avoid contact in an effort not to be touched and hide in closed off areas

- Is your dog sleeping a lot more and becoming inactive?

- Have you noticed his overall general health diminish?

- Does your dog still have control over his bladder and bowels? Incontinence is a condition that affects senior dogs in particular. They may be too weak to make it outside, and while incontinence alone may not be a sign your dog is coming to the end of his life, it's time to talk to the vet

- Breathing problems can occur as the body begins to shut down. Problems at the end of a dog's life can show themselves in the form of a chronic cough or the inability to take a deep breath

- Does your Great Dane appear, sound, or act upset, uncomfortable, or distressed for the majority of the time?

- Loss or lack of coordination is commonplace in senior dogs who are nearing the end. Your Great Dane may appear unsteady and clumsy on his feet. He may appear dizzy or bump into things. You may notice that, more and more, he is choosing to be sedentary when he realizes that standing leads to disorientation and loss of control over his limbs.

- Is your dog having difficulty standing? This problem is often caused by pain or muscle weakness and can result in your dog, despite his best efforts, being unable to walk or stand. He may attempt to get up on all four paws only to collapse

- When your Great Dane can no longer do three or more out of his five favorite things, it may be time to say goodbye. Favorite things could include playing Frisbee, eating, or greeting you when you return home. Make a list and be honest with yourself: is your dog's quality of life far less than it should be?

These questions are ones that you must answer honestly. While you may want your local veterinarian to make the choice for you, the final responsibility is yours and yours alone.

Why? Because although the vet can help you with advice on how healthy your dog is, or when old age is too much bear, only you understand any changes in his overall behavior.

Photo Courtesy of Elizabeth Moore

Crossing the Rainbow Bridge: The Final Journey

The decision to bring an end to your Great Dane's suffering is not an easy one to make. It is the most painful part of being a dog owner.

Remember, when faced with this terrible choice, you must put your dog's needs above your own emotions. Once it has been made, rest assured that your veterinarian will be by your side along the way.

His team will assist you in arranging euthanasia. They will explain the process and the procedure to you, and make you aware of any aftercare options available.

The procedure generally consists of two shots, the first being a sedative to put your dog into a deep sleep. This shot is followed by the second injection that will cause your dog's heart to slow before finally stopping.

You will have the opportunity to be present during this procedure, which is peaceful and pain-free. This is your choice. There is no right answer and your vet will no doubt support you whatever you decide.

It may be possible for your vet to visit you at home and carry out the procedure there rather than at the surgery. When our first rescue Great Dane, Arnold, was too ill to even stand, let alone eat, we chose this option. As heartbreaking as it was, we both sat together under his favorite tree in the garden, and he slipped away peacefully in our arms.

For however long your Great Dane has been a part of your family, he no doubt will forever hold a special place in your heart.

There are a number of ways to honor his life.

The most common are:

- Home Burial
- Communal Cremation
- Private Cremation

Getting over the loss of a pet can be a huge struggle.

Everyone grieves differently, and if your family is made up of young children or teens, it may take a lot of patience and support.

You are not alone though; many other Great Dane owners have traveled this unwanted path and gone on, in time, to welcome another gentle giant into their home to steal their hearts.

CPSIA information can be obtained
at www.ICGtesting.com
Printed in the USA
BVHW021718100920
588446BV00003B/19